•COOL DEVOTIONS FOR GUYS•

GOTTA HAVE GOD

AGES 10-12

LEGACY PRESS®
www.LegacyPressKids.com

•COOL DEVOTIONS FOR GUYS•

GOTTA HAVE GOD

AGES 10-12

Linda Washington
&
Jeanette Dall

*For my grandson, Matthew, one of God's beloved sons,
who will someday be able to read this. — JAD*

For my nephews, Samuel Preston Washington and Joseph Donermeyer. — LMW

GOTTA HAVE GOD FOR AGES 10-12
©2014 by Legacy Press, twenty-sixth printing
ISBN 10: 1-885358-98-9
ISBN 13: 978-1-885358-98-1
Legacy reorder #LP46963
JUVENILE NONFICTION / Religion / Devotion & Prayer

Legacy Press
P.O. Box 261129
San Diego, CA 92196
www.LegacyPressKids.com

MIX
Paper from
responsible sources
FSC® C013572

Interior Illustrator: Aline L. Heiser
Cover Illustrator: Helen Harrison

Unless otherwise noted, Scriptures are from the *Holy Bible: New International Version*
(North American Edition), copyright ©1973, 1978, 1984 by the International Bible Society.
Used by permission of Zondervan Bible Publishers.

Scripture quotations marked NLT are from the *Holy Bible, New Living Translation*, copyright
©1996. Used by permission of Tyndale House Publishers, Inc., Wheaton, Illinois 60189. All
rights reserved.

Printed in South Korea

TABLE OF CONTENTS

TABLE OF CONTENTS

TABLE OF CONTENTS

INTRODUCTION

Hey, guys, did you know that Jesus wants to be your best friend? This book can help you learn more about Him! Jesus knows all about being a guy because He was one. If you are like most guys, there is stuff in your life that needs God's help. That's what's really cool about this book. As you read each devotion, you will find out more about God and how to be a Christian. After you read, there is a fun activity to help you understand the Bible.

You can read the devotionals in this book whenever you want and in whatever order you like. Each one has a topic and a Scripture. Try to memorize the Scriptures! Then there is a story and some questions that will make you think. Write some of your answers on the lines below the questions. After your prayer, take a look at the activity. The projects and puzzles will help you act on what you've just learned. At the back of the book, you will find answers to the puzzles (not that you'll need them!).

When you get ready to read one of the devotionals, find a quiet place where you can relax. Bring your Bible and a pencil. You might want to draw a line under Scriptures in your Bible that you really like.

You're gonna be amazed at how much you Gotta Have God!

ALL ABOUT ME

WHO AM I?

I am God's child.
I have summoned you by name; you are mine.

Isaiah 43:1

A Special Name

Robert Samuels was reading an article about famous sports people of the 1900's. "Listen to these neat names," he said to his dad. "Air Jordan. Slammin' Sammy. Big Mac. Crazy Legs. The Greatest."

Dad smiled as he thought about those athletes. He even went on to name a few others that he remembered. Robert rested his chin on his hands and sighed, "I wish I had a special name — one that tells everyone who I am."

His sister, Tammy, had some suggestions, "How about Boring Bob or Recap Robert, because you say everything twice. Or maybe Slow-Poke Samuels would be better."

Robert glared at Tammy. "Oh, right! Then we'll just call you Tattletale Tammy or Scatterbrain Samuels!"

"OK! Enough already!" Dad said. "Name calling is off limits!" Both kids made one final face at each other before they started grinning.

Dad said to Robert, "You were named for your great grandfather, the first mayor of this town. But you know what? You're forgetting all about your best name. That's the name God calls you. He calls you His child: a Christian."

Then Dad whispered, "I had a special name when I played basketball, Foul-Happy Fred, but I think I'd rather forget that one!"

Robert nodded his head in agreement.

Your Turn

1. What is special about your name?
2. What is special about being called God's child? What does it mean?

_____

_____

_____

_____

Prayer

God, thank You for making me Your child. Help me always to be proud of being a Christian. Amen.

WHAT ARE YOU CALLED?

How many names and nicknames do you have? Write down as many as you can think of.

_____

_____

Which is your favorite name? _____

Do you know what your name means? _____

You may be called other names that tell who you are or what you do. Circle the names that apply to you, then fit all of the names into the puzzle. When you are finished, the letters in the boxes will spell one more name. The answers are on page 243.

ARTIST   **ATHLETE**   **NEPHEW**

SON   **COUSIN**   **BROTHER**

GRANDSON **FRIEND**   **STUDENT**

My most important name is __ __ __ __ __ __ __ __.

WHO AM I?

I was created in God's image.
So God created man in his own image.

Genesis 1:27

You Look Just Like...

The Hernandez family had just arrived at the annual family picnic. Suddenly, a woman came running up and hugged Mrs. Hernandez. "Ellen, I'm so glad you came," the woman said. "Your son sure looks like you — same freckles, same hair. Catch ya later." She hurried off.

"Cousin Rosie," Mrs. Hernandez explained to her husband, who seemed amused by the scene.

Just then a man shook his hand. "Welcome, Bill," the man said. "Good to see you." Then he looked at Hector and said, "Wow! You sure look like your Dad — same eyes, same nose."

"That's Uncle Ben," Mr. Hernandez explained to Hector.

At noon, Hector took his loaded plate and sat next to Grandpa. "I'm sure getting tired of people saying I look like Mom or Dad. I'm me!"

Grandpa Hernandez gave a hearty laugh and then he said, "Sure you're you, but you're a little bit of your Mom and Dad too. You even have some of me in you. All the relatives here are alike in some way or another because we're all from the same family.

"Actually, all the people in the world are alike in one way. They're all made in the image of God. That means we share God's nature and can love, be wise, be truthful and enjoy all the wacky relatives He gives us."

Hector laughed and dug into his food.

Your Turn

1. Whom do people say you look like?
2. Why is it important that we're made in the "image of God"?

_____

_____

_____

_____

Prayer

God, help me to remind others of You when they see how I act and hear what I say. Amen.

FAMILY COAT OF ARMS

Years ago, families had "coats of arms." These were on shields or tunics worn by soldiers. A coat of arms let everyone know about the person's family who wore it. The coat of arms showed the family name, a motto and some symbols that told the family's business or why the family was famous. Make a coat of arms for your family. Your last name goes in the center. Then think of a short motto for your family and some symbols that tell about your family. Some ideas: cross, books, animals, heart (love), sports, etc.

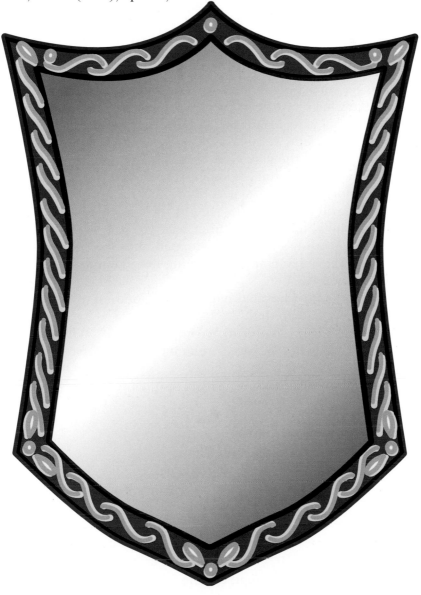

WHO AM I?

My actions show others that I am a child of God.
*I am the good shepherd; I know my sheep
and my sheep know me.*

John 10:14

Remember Who You Are

Andy slammed his locker shut and set off for home. At the school door, a group of boys caught up with him. They were laughing and joking as they headed outside. Andy stepped out of their way.

"Hey, Andy," one of the boys said, "wanna come over to Jerry's house and see something?"

Andy was so surprised that Scott even talked to him, that he just mumbled, "Like what?"

"It's a really cool video: Main Street Murders," said Jerry. "My brother told me to return it, but we're going to watch it first." The other boys cheered as Jerry pulled the video out of his backpack.

"Bet there's lots of shooting, blood and gore," said Scott. "Hurry up, we need to see it before Jerry's mom gets home. Just say you had to stay after school — no one will ever know."

Remember who you are. Remember who you are. The words seemed to be screaming in Andy's brain. He stopped and told the boys, "I can't come with you. That's lying and disobeying my parents. Count me out." Then he headed home.

Andy told his mom what had happened. "Good for you!" his mother said. "It took courage to do that."

"I remembered what Dad said," Andy replied. " 'When you face a problem, remember who you are.' I remembered I am part of the Reilly family and we don't lie or disobey."

"You're part of God's family too," his mother reminded Andy. "God's children don't lie or disobey either."

Your Turn

1. Why might Andy want to go with the boys?
2. How do you think he felt after he said "no"?

Prayer

Dear God, help me always remember who I am — Your child. Amen.

WHO YOU ARE

Christians are called by lots of names in the Bible. Many of these names tell who you are. See if you can find these names in the puzzle below. The answer is on page 243.

believer (Acts 4:32)

child [of God] (John 1:12)

Christian (Acts 11:26)

fisher (Matthew 4:19)

friend (John 15:14)

lamb (John 21:15)

branch (John 15:5)

chosen (1 Peter 2:9)

disciple (John 8:31)

follower (John 12:26)

heir (Romans 8:17)

sheep (John 10:15)

```
M B R A N C H E I R T
S H E L P I C S I D F
H C W L C H O S E N I
E C H R I S T I A N S
E E N I F E E V O L H
P A U L L O V G R A E
F R I E N D L E P M R
D F O L L O W E R B S
```

MY TALENTS AND GIFTS

God has given everyone gifts and talents.
It is the one and only Holy Spirit who distributes these gifts. He alone decides which gift each person should have.
1 Corinthians 12:11, NLT

The No-Hitter

"You shoulda seen me today!" Rick O'Neal yelled, as he ran in the house. "I pitched a no-hitter!"

"All right!" his father slapped hands with him.

"Nobody could touch me! I told Austin Campbell I could do it. I'm a better pitcher than him any day."

"Well, Mr. Cool, I'm sure you've heard of the word 'sportsmanship.'"

"Yeah, yeah. But you gotta admit, Dad, I'm a better pitcher than Austin."

"Well, I'd like you to admit something."

"What?"

"That God is the one who gave you that talent. Knowing that God is the one who gives us good gifts and talents can keep us from..." his father cleared his throat "...getting a big head."

"Aw, Dad! Can't I brag a little?"

"You can be happy about doing something well. But boasting about it isn't cool. Would you like it if someone told you he's a better pitcher than you?"

"Well, I'd know he was lying," Rick grinned.

Mr. O'Neal grabbed him in a mild head lock. Rick laughed and cried "Uncle."

Your Turn

1. What abilities do you have?
2. How can you use your abilities for God?

_____

_____

_____

_____

Prayer

God, help me appreciate the gifts and talents You have given me. Amen.

MEN OF GOD

God worked through many people in the Bible. The men below all had a special purpose. Answers can be found across, down, diagonally and backward. In this puzzle, "John" must be found separately. It is not part of "John Mark." The answer is on page 243.

Aaron	Josiah	Abraham	Matthew
David	Moses	Ezra	Nathan
Isaiah	Noah	James	Pastor
John	Paul	John Mark	Peter
Jonathan	Philip	Joseph	

```
P  I  L  I  H  P  E  S  O  J
J  N  U  E  S  V  J  B  A  O
O  D  A  T  K  A  W  H  B  N
S  I  P  T  M  E  I  A  R  A
I  V  A  E  H  N  Z  A  A  T
A  A  S  T  T  A  I  R  H  H
H  D  T  J  I  E  N  O  A  A
H  A  O  N  T  X  R  N  M  N
M  H  R  M  O  S  E  S  V  O
N  K  R  A  M  N  H  O  J  Q
```

MY TALENTS AND GIFTS

No gift or ability is better than another.
Now you are the body of Christ, and each one of you is a part of it.
1 Corinthians 12:27

Anything You Can Do

The kids in Mr. Simmons' Sunday school class were in the middle of setting up for a skit. The boys had volunteered to help build the stage backdrop. They didn't want the girls to help.

"What can you girls do?" Ryan asked.

"We can do anything you can do," Stephanie said. "Anyway, I'd rather paint the backdrop."

"Building it is more important. Besides, you can't even hammer a nail straight."

"Oh, what do you know?"

"I know I'm not hearing you two argue over which job is better," Mr. Simmons said.

Ryan and Stephanie had not realized their teacher stood near them.

"He started it!" Stephanie accused.

"This is supposed to be fun," Mr. Simmons said. He folded his arms. "When we all work together, no job is more important than another. Just like no ability God gives us is better than an ability He gave to someone else. Isn't that right, Ryan?" He stared at Ryan.

"I was just teasing her," Ryan said, with a foolish grin.

"Let's you and me take a time-out and talk about this teasing."

Stephanie took the hammer from Ryan. "I'll handle this until you get back," she said with a grin.

Your Turn

1. Think about the talents you have. How do you see those abilities? (Circle one. Be honest!)
   - I'm better than anyone else at what I do.
   - I'm no better than anyone else.
   - Haven't thought about it yet.
2. How do you think God wants you to see those abilities?

Prayer

Lord, help me see my abilities the way You do. Amen.

PAPER PINBALL

To play this paper pinball game, you don't need coins. You just need knowledge. To launch your first ball through the game, circle the names of people who were prophets of God. To launch your second ball through the game, put a square around the names of people God gave the ability to do miraculous things like heal people. Warning: One name doesn't fit either category. Some names fit both. For each correct answer, give yourself 5 points. The answer is on page 243.

PEOPLE IN MY LIFE

God gave me the family I have.
Be devoted to each other in brotherly love.

Romans 12:10

Little Brother

"And stay OUTTA my room!" Kent yelled, with a final slam of his door. *That'll teach him!* he thought. *Little brothers! What a pain!*

That was the third time that week Kent had caught his six-year-old brother, Petey, in his room snooping around his stuff.

Suddenly his glance fell on a folded piece of blue construction paper on his pillow. He recognized Petey's writing. Petey had made a card for him.

"My big brother is kool." Petey had misspelled cool, but Kent knew what he meant. Kent opened the card. "I know you are sad about your bad grade. I hope you feel better."

Kent shook his head. He had been in a foul mood because of the bad grade he had received on his science quiz. He suddenly felt sad that he had gotten so angry at Petey. Petey was a pain, but he did like to do things to cheer up others.

Kent threw open his door. "Hey, Petey!" he called. He found Petey playing with a construction set on the floor. "I'm sorry I yelled at you," he said. "Wanna go play a computer game with me?"

Petey's look brightened. "Yeah!"

Kent breathed a silent prayer, *Thank God for my little brother.*

Your Turn

1. In what ways are you thankful for the people in your family?
2. When was the last time you told the people in your family what they mean to you?

_____

_____

_____

_____

_____

Prayer

Thank You, God, for my family. Amen.

YOUR MISSION

Your mission, should you decide to accept it, is to show concern for others. "How?" you may say. Glad you asked. Cross out the Xs, Qs, and Ds. The answer is on page 243.

PEOPLE IN MY LIFE

God brings many people into my life.
God sets the lonely in families.

Psalm 68:6

Miss Velma

"Tyrice, get ready. I want you to go with me to Miss Velma's," Mrs. Robinson said.

Tyrice groaned. "Do I have to, Mom? She always calls me Bernard." Bernard was his brother.

"You know she likes to see young people in her house. She gets lonely for company. Besides, she's like family."

"She's old. And she smells funny."

"Tyrice, you know I don't like you talking about her like that."

"It's true, Mom."

"I know. But we're all the family Miss Velma has. She was my grandmother's best friend. Miss Velma's like a grandmother to me. I'm grateful to God we still have her. You know she thinks the world of you. She's done some nice things for you, hasn't she?"

Tyrice didn't want to admit that. Miss Velma never forgot to send him a birthday present or a Christmas present. Yet he always grumbled whenever his mother made him give her a card. Suddenly, he felt ashamed.

"Hey, Mom, can we swing by the grocery store?" he asked, on their way out.

"What for?"

"I wanna get Miss Velma a plant or something. Think I can find one for under $3?"

Mrs. Robinson smiled and quickly hugged Tyrice before he could escape.

Your Turn

1. Name someone you feel close to in your neighborhood or at church.
2. How can you let that person know that he or she is special to you?

Prayer

Thank You, Lord, for giving me so many people to care about and who care about me. Amen.

FAMILY RELATIONS

Fit each of the following words into the puzzle below. The words are arranged below alphabetically according to the number of letters. The answer is on page 243.

4 Letters
aunt

5 Letters
coach
uncle

6 Letters
friend
cousin
father
mother
pastor
sister

7 Letters
brother
teacher

11 Letters
grandfather

13 Letters
choir
director

PEOPLE IN MY LIFE

God put certain leaders in my life.
Obey your leaders and submit to their authority.
Hebrews 13:17

Respect

Rodney knew he was in for it when he saw his uncle's face.

"Rodney, what's this I hear about you yelling at your basketball coach?" Uncle James asked when he arrived to pick up Rodney from practice.

"Dennis Rodman does it all the time," Rodney said. He liked Dennis Rodman.

"You know better. I just had a long talk with your coach. He's ready to keep you on the bench for pulling a stunt like that."

"He just doesn't like me!" Rodney burst out. "He never says anything to anyone else. Just me. He got mad at me 'cause I wouldn't pass the ball to his son. His son can't shoot!"

"Rod, I know you've been having some trouble with your coach. But remember what we've been talking about? God gives us people in authority over us. That means they deserve our respect. You know what this means, don't you?"

Rodney had some idea, but wanted to play dumb. "No."

"You owe your coach an apology."

Rodney groaned, but knew his uncle wouldn't allow him to refuse for long. Besides, he knew his uncle was right.

Your Turn

1. Who are the leaders in your life?
2. How do you show them respect?
3. Why is it important to show respect to those in authority?

_____

_____

_____

_____

_____

Prayer

Lord, I need Your help to respect the leaders in my life. Amen.

THE ULTIMATE LEADER

Fill in the name of each leader to find the name of the ultimate leader. The answers are on page 243.

1. The person ranked above a captain, but below a lieutenant colonel.
2. The leader of your class at school.
3. Each state elects two of these leaders.
4. The leader of a courtroom.
5. The leader of your church.

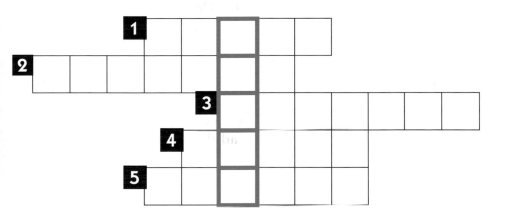

PEOPLE IN MY LIFE

God wants me to be kind to my neighbors.
*Do not be proud, but be willing to associate
with people of low position.*

Romans 12:16

Next Door Neighbor

Chris sighed. He had heard it all before from his mother: "Why is it you never invite the boy next door to do anything?" Blah, blah. There she stood in his room saying the same thing. Could he help it if Reginald wasn't cool? It wasn't his decision. The other kids in the sixth grade had decided it. Chris was just going along with how everyone else felt about Reginald.

If only Reginald were better at sports. He couldn't dribble a basketball to save his life. And baseball? Well, just forget that! Chris was good at both. He was also (if he said so himself!) fairly well liked by everyone. Yeah, too bad about Reginald.

Chris ignored the nagging feeling in the back of his mind. He tried to ignore the feeling that he ought to make an effort to be kinder to Reginald. Lately, the feeling had been getting stronger and stronger. Whenever Chris thought about God and what God had done for him, he noticed that feeling. *Oh, well*, he thought.

Your Turn

1. What do you think Chris could do to be kinder to Reginald?
2. Is there a "Reginald" in your life? What could you do to show kindness to that person?

_____

_____

_____

_____

Prayer

Dear God, show me how to be kind to others. Amen.

KINDNESS MULTIPLE CHOICE

Who showed kindness? If you can name the person who showed kindness, you get that amount of points, just as if you had thrown a dart. The point squares are numbered to match the questions. The answers are on page 244.

1. Jesus' told the story of a man who was kind to a man who had been robbed. Who was he?
   (a) a Levite; (b) a priest; (c) a Samaritan (Luke 10:25-37)

2. Who showed kindness to Jonathan's son Mephibosheth?
   (a) David; (b) Saul; (c) Samuel (2 Samuel 4:4, 9)

3. He showed kindness to his brothers, even though they had treated him unkindly.
   (a) Jonathan; (b) Joseph; (c) Josiah (Genesis 37; 39–50)

4. This woman showed kindness by refusing to leave her mother-in-law, even though she could have stayed in Moab.
   (a) Orpah; (b) Naomi; (c) Ruth

5. When this woman showed kindness to Abraham's servant, he knew that she was the woman God chose to became Isaac's wife.
   (a) Rebekah; (b) Rachel; (c) Ruth

6. This man showed kindness to David by just being his friend.
   (a) Saul; (b) Jonathan; (c) Samuel

7. Who showed kindness to Ruth by letting her glean in his field?
   (a) Barnabas; (b) Bartholomew; (c) Boaz

8. This young man did not want to show kindness to the older people in his kingdom. After that, the kingdom of Israel became divided.
   (a) Jeroboam; (b) Rehoboam; (c) Solomon

9. Peter brought this woman, who showed kindness to widows, back to life.
   (a) Miriam; (b) Dorcas; (c) his mother-in-law (Acts 9:36-42)

MY MAJOR PROBLEMS

FEAR

God helps me face my fears.
So do not fear, for I am with you...
I will strengthen you and help you.

Isaiah 41:10

Kevin's Fear

Kevin felt silly. *I don't have to be afraid. I don't have to be afraid*, he said to himself over and over. Yet he was afraid. Of what? He made a face as he thought about it. He was so afraid of not winning, of making his Little League team look bad. He had done that before. His teammates had gotten angry the last time he struck out.

He felt tense as he thought about next Saturday's game. *What if I strike out again?* he thought. It almost made his stomach hurt.

"Why are you looking like that?" his older brother Derek asked. "You worried about Saturday's game?"

"How did you know?" Kevin asked.

"You've been quiet ever since the last game."

"I just don't want to strike out." Kevin felt a little better just admitting it.

"Why don't you pray about it?" Derek asked. "I'm not saying ask God to help you not strike out. I'm saying, you can ask God to help you not be afraid and do your best. I've done that lots of times."

Kevin grinned. "Maybe you're not so dumb after all."

Your Turn

1. What was Kevin afraid of? How do you think his brother's advice will help?
2. What are you afraid of? How can you follow Derek's advice?

_____

_____

_____

_____

_____

Prayer

Lord, I'm afraid of _____ (fill in the blank). Please help me overcome this fear. Amen.

FEAR FIGHTER

Want a way to face your fears? Solve the rebus to find out. Some words are sound-alikes. The answer is on page 244.

 -T   Y+

_____

 -CK    - AR

_____

IN  -AL    -TOA

_____

FEAR

God is with me when I am afraid.
*Even though I walk through the valley of the shadow
of death, I will fear no evil, for you are with me; your
rod and your staff, they comfort me.*

Psalm 23:4

The Red Dogs

Shawn James looked at the elevator down the hall from the apartment he lived in. The gang that hung around the building had marked it with graffiti. Shawn shook his head. Some of the members of the Red Dogs gang had asked him to join the gang a week ago. So far, Shawn had avoided running into them. But how long would it be before they asked him again?

That horrible feeling of fear clutched at him. Shawn's friend Trey had been beaten up for not joining the gang. Shawn and Trey had both become Christians at the church near where they lived. Would Shawn be next to get beaten up? Shawn had prayed many times for God's help. Would He answer?

"Hey, Shawn," Ross, another friend, said as he left his apartment. "Good news, man. Police busted most of the Dogs yesterday. Caught 'em stealing stuff out of Mrs. Grey's apartment. They're finally gone!"

Shawn sighed with relief. His fear was gone too!

Your Turn

1. Shawn faced a serious fear. Any fear you have is serious to you. What do you usually do when you're afraid?
2. What support can your family or friends offer when you're afraid?
3. How has God helped you face fears in the past?

_____

_____

_____

_____

_____

Prayer

Lord, I don't like being afraid. But sometimes I am. Please help me face my fears. Amen.

FEAR LIFTER

If you need a guaranteed fear lifter, use the code below to find a message based on Joshua 1:9. The answer is on page 244.

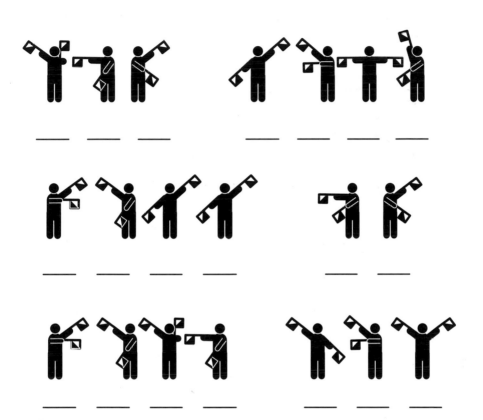

___ ___ ___   ___ ___

___ ___ ___ ___   ___ ___

___ ___ ___ ___   ___ ___ ___

A B C D E H I L M N

O R S T U W X Y

ANGER

I must control my anger or it will control me.
*My dear brothers, take note of this: Everyone should be quick to
listen, slow to speak and slow to become angry.*

James 1:19

Quick to Anger

"Why are you so mad?" Steve asked. He grinned at his big sister Wendy, knowing that a grin would make her even madder.

"Because you make me sick sometimes!" Wendy yelled. "I know you have my Edgy Beavers CD. You're always taking my CDs! You scratched one last week! Scratched!"

"I didn't take anything this time," Steve said.

"Wendy," their mother called from the living room, "come here, please."

Steve trailed after Wendy. He knew that sound in their mother's voice.

Mrs. Hiller held up a CD when they walked in. "This yours?" she asked.

Wendy looked embarrassed as she took the CD from her mother. "Where did you find it?"

"That's not as important as the fact that you keep losing your temper. I heard you all the way in the garage. Remember what I told you about that?"

"Yeah," Wendy muttered.

All the while, Steve had been grinning. Mrs. Hiller's gaze fell on him. "That goes for you too, Steve," she said.

Your Turn

1. Have you ever been quick to get angry at someone? What happened?
2. Why is it better to "be quick to listen, slow to speak and slow to become angry" as James 1:19 says?
3. What can you do instead of yelling at someone in anger?

_____

_____

_____

_____

Prayer

Help me, Lord, to be quick to listen, slow to speak and slow to become angry. Amen.

ANGER ADVICE

Solve the rebus to find some good advice from Proverbs 29:11 about anger. The answers are on page 244.

A  -D+L

FULL  TO HIS -H, BUT A

UNDER -VICT + -L

ANGER

God doesn't want me to hold a grudge.
"In your anger do not sin." Do not let the sun
go down while you are still angry.

Ephesians 4:26

The Grudge

"Why are you so happy?" Jason asked his friend Colin.

"I'm finally the team captain in street hockey," Colin said. "I can get back at Bruce for choosing me last when he was team captain."

"What're you gonna do?" Jason asked.

"Not choose him. I told Alex, the other team captain, to wait 'til everybody's chosen to pick him if he wants." Colin looked pleased with himself. "Bruce's gonna look stupid."

"Man, you know that's not right," Jason said.

Colin rolled his eyes. "Here we go."

"What?" Jason asked.

"You're gonna talk about religion. I just know it."

Jason sighed. He invited Colin to Sunday school several times. Sometimes Colin went and sometimes he didn't. He also knew Colin was one to hold a grudge.

"I know you're still mad at Bruce," Jason said. "But what's getting back at him gonna do? You won't feel better."

Colin gave Jason a look. "Later," he said.

Jason sighed again. *I know I did the right thing in telling him*, he thought.

Your Turn

1. Was Colin right to get even? Why or why not?
2. What happens when you try to get even with someone?

_____

_____

_____

_____

Prayer

God, I think about _____ (fill in the situation that bothers you right now). Help me do the right thing. Amen.

GET IT? GOT IT? GOOD!

Instead of getting even with someone who makes you mad, here are some things to "get" instead:

Get:
* wisdom (James 1:5)
*with God in prayer (Matthew 6:13)
*rid of thoughts of revenge (Hebrews 10:30-31)

SADNESS

Death is not sad because I know Jesus.
He will wipe every tear from their eyes.
Revelation 21:4

Missing Gramps

Jared sat scrunched up, his head in his hands. He was trying to pretend that nothing had changed. Jared was so upset that he didn't hear his mother come into the room. She put a big box next to Jared.

"I went to Gramps's house today and sorted through some of his belongings," she said gently. "I brought home some things I thought you might like to have. You can look at them when you feel like it." Then his mother left the room.

I'll never feel like it! Jared thought. He sobbed as he thought about Gramps's sudden death from a heart attack. One day his grandfather was laughing and joking with Jared and the next day he was dead.

After a while, Jared glanced at the box his mother had left. The Chinese checkers board and a jar of marbles were sticking out of the top. When his mom came in with a snack, she found Jared holding the marble jar.

"It helps me feel better to hold these," Jared whispered. "They help me remember all the games Gramps and I played. But I miss him so much! Things will never be the same without him."

His mom hugged Jared. "I know. And it's OK to cry and feel sad. You loved Gramps a lot. But you know what? Things have changed for Gramps, too, because he's in heaven with Jesus now. Everything is perfect there and he's very happy."

Thinking of Gramps in heaven made Jared smile a bit.

Your Turn

1. Has anyone you loved died? How did you feel?
2. What do you think heaven will be like?

_____

_____

_____

_____

Prayer

Lord, please help me when I'm sad. And help me comfort others who are sad. Amen.

HEAVEN IS A WONDERFUL PLACE

No one knows for sure what heaven will be like. Think of the most beautiful or perfect place you've ever been. Then think of the place where you feel the happiest. Heaven will be a thousand times better than either of those places! Draw a picture or write about your idea of heaven.

Heaven

SADNESS

God can help me overcome my sad time.
[There is] a time to weep and a time to laugh.

Ecclesiastes 3:4

Feeling Miserable

Scott slammed the kitchen door so hard that the cat went running and his mother jumped. He dumped his backpack on the chair, stomped upstairs and flung himself across the bed. He covered his face with his pillow.

Scott's mom came into his room. "I take it you had a bad day," she said. All she heard was a muffled grunt. "Do you want to talk about it?" she asked.

Scott removed the pillow and sighed. "It was a rotten afternoon," he blurted. "I'll never be able to face the sixth grade boys or coach again."

"And why is that?" his mom asked.

Scott took a deep breath. "We had a basketball game against Edison Middle School and we were ahead by two points. Then I got the ball, raced down the court, and made a perfect lay up. Everybody was yelling and I thought they were cheering for me."

"That's bad?" Mom asked.

"Yeah, when you put it in the wrong basket," Scott mumbled. "I was so embarrassed! How could I be so stupid?"

"I can see why you feel miserable," said his mom. "You may feel sad for awhile, but you'll be happy again. Even God says that's the way things happen. Something that works for me when I'm sad is to help someone else. Then I forget about myself. Your brother would love to learn how to shoot baskets."

At least I won't get it in the wrong basket, Scott thought as he went to find Jimmy.

Your Turn

1. How do you get over feeling sad?
2. How can God help you when you're sad?

Prayer

God, thanks for being with me all the time—even when I'm miserable. Amen.

HAPPY/SAD

Fit these happy or sad words into the puzzle. The answers are on page 244.

DOWN
EXCITED
GROAN
LAUGHING
MOPE
MOURN
SAD
SOB
WHIMPER

ACROSS
CRYING
GIGGLE
GLAD
HAPPY
JOYFUL
MISERABLE
POUT
SINGING
SMILE

WORRY

God is in control of the future, so I don't have to worry.
I will instruct you and teach you in the way you should go.
I will counsel you and watch over you.

Psalm 32:8

Divorce Worry

"So what do you worry about?" Sid asked during a break in his turn at the joystick. He waited while the computer game reset itself.

"I worry about not getting a turn," his brother Carl said.

"I'm serious." Sid surrendered the joystick. "I heard Mom and Dad fighting yesterday. They must've thought we couldn't hear them. Do you ever worry that they'll get a divorce or something?"

Carl glanced at him. "They've fought before."

"Lamar's parents are getting a divorce." Lamar lived two doors away.

"Oh." Carl paused. "Well, I've even heard Lamar's parents fighting. They never seemed to even like each other." He concentrated on the game for a bit before he spoke again. "Mom and Dad aren't like that."

"Yeah, I guess…"

"Maybe you should talk to them instead of worrying about it."

Sid stared at Carl. What his brother said made sense. He had heard that God sometimes spoke through people. But he never expected God to speak through his younger brother!

Your Turn

1. What worries you right now?
2. What do you usually do when you're worried?

_____

_____

_____

_____

_____

_____

Prayer

God, I'm worried about _____ (fill in your concern): I'm not sure what to do. Please help me know what to do. Amen.

ZAP THOSE WORRIES

Wouldn't it be great if you could zap your worries as easily as you zap space aliens in a video game? With God's Word, you can cut those worries down to size. Check out the worries on the left. Are any of these your worries? Which of the following verses from the power grid would you use to defeat those worries? Draw a line from the worry to the Scripture that would help it. The answers are on page 244.

WORRY

God can help me face the problems that worry me.
My times are in your hands.

Psalm 31:15a

Best Friend Worry

"Jan, you still staring at the wall?" Michael asked. "Earth to Jan...Houston, we've got a problem."

"Funny." Jan didn't feel much like laughing. "Christine's mad at me again."

"So what else is new?" Michael paused to laugh.

"It's not funny."

Michael finally stopped laughing when he saw how worried his sister looked. "She's never been a good friend. Lose her. You don't need her."

"She's my best friend. Or was." Jan looked close to tears. "I don't know what to do."

Michael leaned against the wall. "What are you worried about?"

Jan shrugged. "I don't know what I did wrong this time."

"But what are you really worried about?" Michael looked at her closely. "There's got to be more to it."

"Christine's really popular. If I'm not friends with her..." Jan didn't want to think of what could happen.

Michael waved his hand. "Don't worry."

"Easy for you to say."

"Easier to do than worry. What about trusting that God's in control? Didn't you tell me that last week?" Michael grinned at Jan.

Your Turn

1. What was Jan worried about?
2. Have you ever had a worry like that? What did you do?

_____

_____

_____

_____

Prayer

Thank You, God for being in control of my life. Amen.

BIG WHACK ATTACK

Need a secret weapon to whack those worries? Here's one that's not so secret. To discover it, you'll need to put this puzzle together. You can photocopy this page and cut the pieces apart, or scan it and print it on your computer. (You'll still need to cut the pieces apart when you print it out.) The answer is on page 244.

WORRY

God wants me to do my best and not worry about the outcome.
Trust in the Lord and do good.

Psalm 37:3a

Learning to Lean

"I can't do this!" Philip Franklin yelled. "This report stinks. That means I'll get another bad grade!"

"What's wrong?" his father asked.

"I don't know if my report on Saturn is good enough to get a good grade."

Mr. Franklin put his hand on Philip's shoulder as he read what was on the computer screen. "I know you've tried your best."

"I've been studying, Dad. I thought I was doing better." Philip felt almost ready to cry in frustration. He had been getting extra help at school, now that everyone knew that he had a problem learning. He worried that the problem would last forever.

"I don't think your report is as bad as you think," Mr. Franklin said. "Your teacher will understand. Your grades have gotten better. But this isn't something to worry yourself sick over. I wish you didn't have to go through this, son. Your mother and I pray for you every day. We know God is helping you right now to learn to lean on Him."

"Thanks, Dad." Philip wasn't always sure that God cared about the problem. But right then, he felt better.

Your Turn

1. Is there a problem that worries you right now? On whom do you rely to help when you have a problem?
2. Why doesn't worrying about the problem help?
3. How can you show that you trust God to take care of your problem?

_____

_____

_____

_____

Prayer

Lord, instead of worrying, help me trust You. Amen.

WHAT, ME WORRY?

The opposite of worry is trust. "But trust in what?" you may ask. Solve the puzzle below to see a message from Psalm 119:42. Starting at the letter indicated, write every other letter. You'll go around the circle clockwise twice. The answer is on page 244.

WORRY

God wants me to live one day at a time, instead of worrying.
Therefore do not worry about tomorrow, for tomorrow will worry
about itself. Each day has enough trouble of its own.

Matthew 6:34

The Letter, Part 1

"I'm dead," Kiyoshi said.

"You...look like you're still alive to me," his friend Wanda said. She had come over to play games on Kiyoshi's computer.

Kiyoshi just looked at her for a second. "Mr. Fletcher wants to see Mom and me in his office tomorrow." Mr. Fletcher was the principal of their school.

"What did you do this time?" Wanda knew that Kiyoshi was famous around school for his practical jokes.

Kiyoshi shrugged. "I don't know. Mom says she received a letter in the mail. She wouldn't tell me anything. She said we'd find out tomorrow."

"You think it's something bad?"

"Got to be. But what though? I didn't do anything recently. I can't stop worrying about it."

Wanda shrugged. "My mom always tells me not to worry about stuff. 'Live one day at a time.' " Wanda was good at imitating her mother. "Anyway, that's what God wants us to do."

"But what's that supposed to mean?"

"It means don't worry about what could happen tomorrow. C'mon. Let's play."

Kiyoshi shrugged. "Maybe you're right."

Your Turn

1. What worried Kiyoshi?
2. Sometimes fear of the unknown can cause us to worry. Why is it better to live one day at a time and not worry about tomorrow as the verse above mentions?

Prayer

Lord, help me not to worry about what could happen tomorrow. Amen.

RIDDLE TIME!

Here's a riddle for the worried. What number can you think of to remind you how much you mean to God? (Hint: It is a number between 1 and 20.) The answer is on page 244.

THE BEST I CAN BE

HUMILITY

God wants me to be humble.
Everyone who exalts himself will be humbled, and he who humbles himself will be exalted.

Luke 14:11

The Letter, Part 2

"So, Kiyoshi, what happened in Mr. Fletcher's office?" Wanda asked.

Kiyoshi grinned. "He wants me to start taking advanced math in the fall. He said my test scores are way up."

"Cool. And you thought you were in trouble. So maybe you can help me with my pre-algebra homework? I brought it with me."

Kiyoshi looked at the problems Wanda pointed out. "You mean you can't do this? This stuff is easy."

"Kiyoshi, I know you're smart, but you don't have to act like a jerk about it."

Kiyoshi figured out the first problem, then handed it to Wanda. "See? The answer is n=6(2)." He buffed his fingernails against his shirt. "I am the Math King."

"Glad to see you're so humble about it," his mother said, as she suddenly entered the room. "Yesterday you were worried to death."

"I had nothing to worry about."

"Hey, Math King, I think something's wrong here." Wanda looked closely at the problem. "You said n = 6(2) is the answer, but I thought 14 couldn't be divided by 6 evenly."

Kiyoshi snatched the paper. "Lemme see that." He looked at it closely. "Whoops."

Wanda laughed. "Looks like the Math King just lost his crown."

Your Turn

1. What does it mean to be humble?

_____

2. On a scale of 1 to 10, how important is it for you to be humble? Circle your choice on the line below. (Be honest.)

1	2	3	4	5	6	7	8	9	10
(NOT MUCH)									(A LOT)

Prayer

Lord, I need Your help to be humble. Amen.

THE KEY

Want to know the key to humility? To discover it, put the letters below each column in the boxes above that column. The letters might not be listed in the exact order in which they appear in the quote. Mark off used letters at the bottom. The first letter has been done for you. A letter may only be used once. Words may continue from one line to the next. The black boxes separate the words. The answers are on page 244.

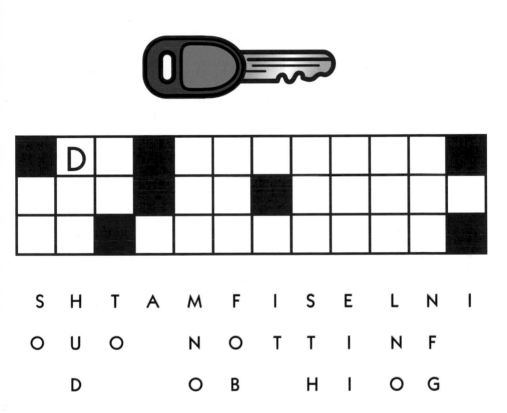

	D											

S	H	T	A	M	F	I	S	E	L	N	I
O	U	O			N	O	T	T	I	N	F
	D			O	B		H	I		O	G

HUMILITY

God wants me to depend on Him, rather than on my own abilities.
I can do everything through him who gives me strength.

Philippians 4:13

The MVP

"Why do you think he said that?"

David turned away from the baseball player on television to look at his father, who had just asked the question.

"Said what?" David replied. "Oh, the stuff about thanking God for making it possible for him to be the MVP? I dunno."

"Take a guess."

David was silent for a moment. "Maybe his father made him do it," he said with a grin. A couch pillow suddenly sailed over his head. "Okay. Maybe he just thought it was a nice thing to do."

"Do you think maybe he was admitting that he depended on God more than on his own ability?"

David shrugged. "Yeah, but he's good, Dad. Nobody pitches like him in the league."

"True. But who gave him that ability in the first place? And anything could have happened to him. He could've been injured during the season. But God kept him from that."

"I guess." David fell silent again. "I never thought about that. I guess maybe...I kinda depend on God too."

"Kinda?!"

David grinned.

Your Turn

1. What talents do you have?
2. Why is it important to think about God, who gave you those abilities?

_____

_____

_____

_____

Prayer

Lord, thank You for giving me the abilities that I have. Amen.

WHO'S NUMBER 1?

If you're a sports fan, how do you show which team is #1 with you? Buy a hat? A T-shirt? How would you tell the world that God is #1? Use the T-shirt or the pennant below to draw or write a slogan that honors God.

LOVE

God helps me love others.
Dear friends, let us love one another, for love comes from God.
Everyone who loves has been born of God and knows God.

1 John 4:7

Grandpa Joe

Brent Carlson slowly walked down the stairs, hoping that his mother had changed her mind. She hadn't. They were still going to visit Grandpa Joe. He sighed as he followed his mother to the garage.

"He always acts like he doesn't like kids," he declared, while strapping himself in.

"I know." His mother started the car.

"So why do I have to go?"

"Because he's your grandfather. Because he's in the hospital." Mrs. Carlson backed out of the garage.

Brent grunted. He thought his grandfather was mean and grouchy. He never seemed to have a kind word to say to anyone.

"I know your grandfather doesn't act very loving sometimes. But that doesn't give us the right to treat him the same way. That's why God helps us love those we have a hard time loving."

Brent grunted again. That's Grandpa for sure!

Your Turn

1. Think of someone you have a hard time loving. How do you usually respond to that person?

2. What do you think God wants you to do? Use the prayer below if you need help.

_____

_____

_____

_____

_____

Prayer

Lord, when it comes to loving some people, I have a hard time doing it. Help me to love those I can't love. Amen.

WHAT IS LOVE?

To find some definitions of love, go through the word maze. If you start at the arrow and keep going through to the period, you'll find a message from 1 Corinthians 13:4. Go for it! The answer is on page 245.

```
O A S T I T I O B
B X L D U O S I E
T N E O . R N T N
O V T O V P O A T
N Y E S N E T P L
S I O ? D N I S O
E T D T I I K S V
O D G N O R W I E
```

LOVE

I should treat myself the way I treat others.
Love your neighbor as yourself.

Matthew 22:39

The Doormat

"I'm sick of being the new kid!" Wesley threw down his backpack as he came in the back door.

His older sister Stephanie laughed. "Is that why you've been letting your so-called friends take advantage of you?" Stephanie, a seventh grader, felt she knew a lot more than Wesley, a mere fifth grader.

"What do you mean?" Wesley asked.

"I saw you at the park today letting that creep Simon ride your new skateboard. He also wrecked it and didn't even say he was sorry. Just threw it back at you and went off with his friends! You should think better of yourself than to let people treat you that way."

"What do you know?" Wesley said.

"I know that I don't want friends like that because that's not the kind of friend I am. I like myself better than that."

"You have to like yourself because nobody else does!" Wesley ran before Stephanie could get him in a headlock.

Your Turn

1. Why is it important to love yourself as well as love your neighbor?
2. Can you ever love yourself too much? Why or why not?
3. What are some ways you can show love to your neighbor? To yourself?

_____

_____

_____

_____

_____

Prayer

Lord, You tell us to love our neighbors as we love ourselves. That's what I want to do. Amen.

LOVE TESTER

Think love is just some oocy gooey feeling? Think again. Take the love tester to see where you stand on the subject of love. On a scale of 1 to 10, how important is it . . .

to forgive someone who has wronged you?

1	2	3	4	5	6	7	8	9	10
(NOT IMPORTANT)								(VERY IMPORTANT)	

to let someone else go first?

1	2	3	4	5	6	7	8	9	10
(NOT IMPORTANT)					(VERY IMPORTANT)				

to help someone you usually don't talk to?

1	2	3	4	5	6	7	8	9	10
(NOT IMPORTANT)				(VERY IMPORTANT)					

If you scored less than 5 on each, take a look at Matthew 5:43-44 and John 13:34-35. What do these verses say about love?

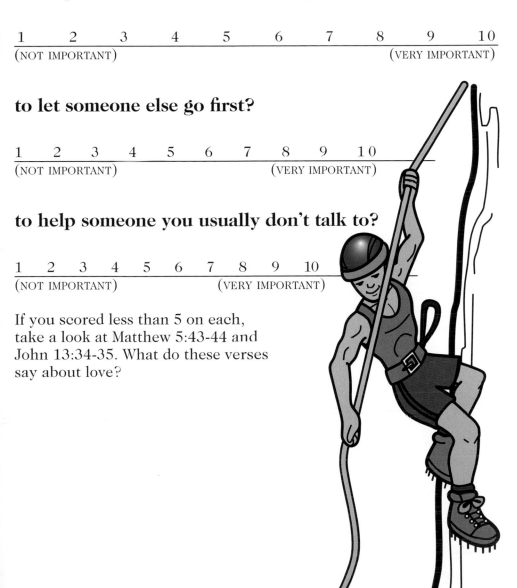

COMPASSION

God gives me grace to show compassion to others.
Show mercy and compassion to one another.

Zechariah 7:9

The Man on the Corner

"Look. See, he's here again." Stuart nudged his cousin Karen and nodded to the homeless man on the corner. He fished around in his pocket for some change to give him.

"Don't give him anything!" Karen hissed. "How do we know he's really homeless? My dad says people sit around out here begging because they don't want to work."

"Yeah, but like I told you, I've seen him here for the past week, now that the weather's warm." Stuart took all of the money out of his pocket and gave it to the man. The man nodded and smiled.

"Hmmph," Karen said. "You just threw your money away. He'll just get drunk with it or something."

Stuart shrugged. "There's nothing wrong with helping people. That's what my Father always says."

"Your dad's dead."

"I'm talking about my heavenly Father. We're only responsible for what we do, not what others do. If I want to be a good Christian, I need to help people. If that man gets drunk with the money I give him, then that's between him and God. Get it?"

Karen thought for a minute. "Maybe you're right," she said as she dug around her pockets for extra change.

Your Turn

1. Do you agree with what Stuart said: "There's nothing wrong with helping people"? Why or why not?
2. Compassion means being moved to act on someone's behalf. It's more than feeling sorry for someone. What person or problem stirs your compassion?

Prayer

When I see someone I can help, I want to show Your compassion. Amen.

COMPASSION.COM

Suppose there were a compassion web site: www.showcompassion.com. If might look something like this:

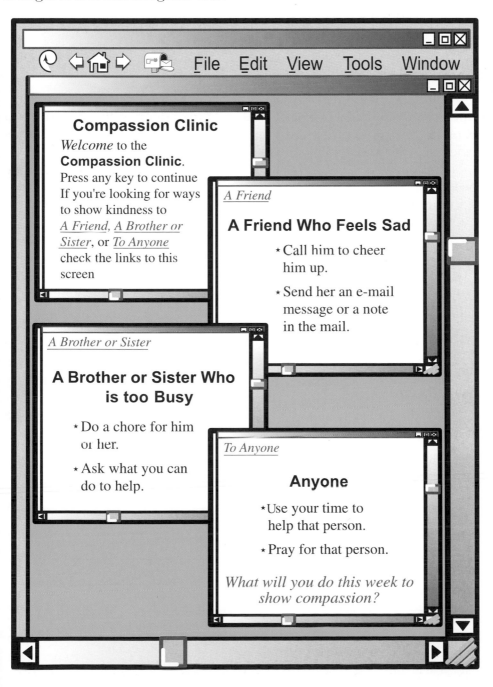

COMPASSION

God wants me to be compassionate.
Be kind and compassionate to one another.
Ephesians 4:32

Help for an Enemy

Paolo Martinez just knew he didn't want to help Dennis. No way! Dennis was a bully. A complete and total menace just like the cartoon character. Hadn't Dennis tried to pick a fight with Paolo? Hadn't Dennis made fun of the way Paolo pitched during gym class?

Now Dennis needed help. Paolo almost couldn't believe it. Dennis needed help in math. He was nearly crying when he asked Paolo for help. "If I don't pass this math test, I'll get a bad grade," Dennis said. He had never seemed to care before.

Paolo was good at math. Everyone knew it. I shouldn't help him, Paolo thought. I should just let him fail.

But then he thought about what God might want him to do. "Love your enemies. Show compassion." He knew compassion was a long word that means "put yourself in someone else's shoes."

Paolo sighed. He couldn't help feeling sorry for Dennis. Dennis tried to act tough and mean, but he had trouble learning sometimes.

Well, Paolo thought, maybe I could help him...this once.

Your Turn

1. How did Paolo show compassion?
2. When has someone shown compassion to you? Why is it important to show compassion?
3. How can you show compassion this week?

_____

_____

_____

_____

_____

Prayer

Jesus, show me someone to care for this week. Amen.

A VERSE TO REMEMBER

The following message can help you show compassion. To discover it, put the letters below each column in the boxes above that column. The letters may not be listed in the exact order in which they appear in the quote. Mark off used letters at the bottom. A letter may only be used once. Words may continue from one line to the next. The black boxes separate words. The answers are on page 245.

JOY

God gives me joy, even when I am sad.
*When morning dawns and evening
fades you call forth songs of joy.*

Psalm 65:8

Buster

Jack looked out his bedroom window. The backyard looked so empty now. He could hardly believe Buster was gone. One minute the little pug chow was there looking at him with those sad eyes. The next minute, there was the vet telling Jack and his family that Buster didn't survive the operation.

He couldn't help thinking how much fun Buster had been. Those thoughts made him feel warm inside.

He soon felt a hand on his shoulder. His mother stood behind him. "I know you're sad, honey," she said.

"Yeah, but I couldn't help remembering how silly Buster is...was." Jack's smile faded.

"Jack, this is part of how life is. We all have to face losses like this. That's why..."

"I know, Mom. God is with us." That's something his mother always said. It was funny though. That thought didn't annoy him this time. This time, he felt glad to know that.

Your Turn

1. What does joy mean to you?
2. Can you think of a time you felt joyful, even though something sad happened?
3. Which lasts longer, joy or happiness? Why?

_____

_____

_____

_____

Prayer

Lord Jesus, You bring me joy. Amen.

WEIRD WORDS

What you see below are familiar phrases presented in a different way. Your job is to figure out what phrase is shown in each case. They can remind you of what God gives you or can help you do. Give yourself the amount of points by each when you guess correctly. The answers are on page 245.

1. 10 points

SJOROROYW

2. 10 points

THE HELP WAY ITS

3. 25 points

JOY BESIDE YOURSELF

Bonus: 50 points

bad bad

good good good good bad good bad

JOY

Knowing Jesus brings me joy.
You have made known to me the path of life; you will fill me with joy in your presence, with eternal pleasures at your right hand.
Psalm 16:11

Read All About It

"What're you grinning at?"

Monica turned when she heard her friend Jay approach her desk. They both had early detention. "I just became—"

"Ssh!" Mr. Keller, the teacher said.

Monica wrote on her notebook and flashed what she wrote to Jay:

I just became a Christian.

Jay wrote a big Y and a question mark on his arm, then grinned.

Monica wrote fast:

Because I finally believe. I know He won't leave me like my dad does. He's always traveling around. I just think it's so cool that Jesus…

Monica suddenly realized that Mr. Keller was standing at her desk. He had his hand out. Monica reluctantly handed over her notebook. "Read chapter 17," Mr. Keller snapped over his shoulder.

Monica glanced at Jay, then slumped in her seat.

Minutes later, Mr. Keller returned her notebook. Monica was surprised to find small writing on it next to hers:

I think Jesus is pretty cool, too.

Monica looked up. Mr. Keller smiled.

Your Turn

1. How would you describe what Monica's relationship with Jesus means to her?
2. How does knowing Jesus bring you joy?
3. If you don't know the joy that knowing Jesus brings but would like to, use this prayer: God, I want to know Your Son, Jesus. I believe He died for my sins. Thank You for the gift of Your Son. Amen.

Prayer

Jesus, I'm glad I know You. Amen.

THE GOSPEL ACCORDING TO YOU

What would you tell a friend about Jesus? The tape recorder is on. Use the speech balloon to record your message.

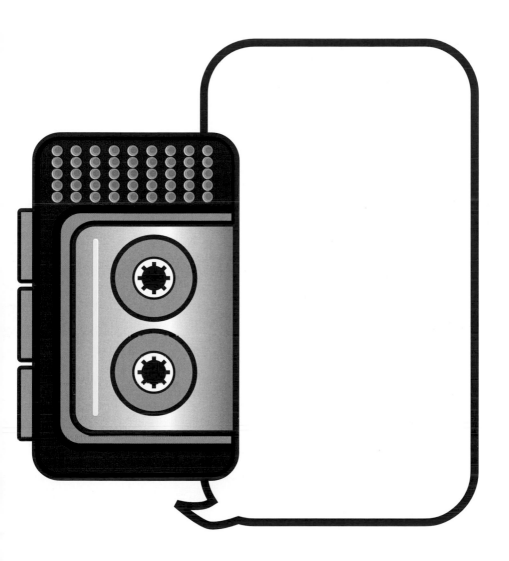

COMMITMENT

When the going gets tough, the committed keep going.
Stand firm. Let nothing move you.
1 Corinthians 15:58

Sticking with It

Alex turned off the lawn mower, then threw down his cap and folded his arms. The large backyard seemed to stretch on forever. Alex's back already hurt from pushing the mower.

"Taking a break already?" his father asked. He looked nice and cool underneath the umbrella on the patio. A glass of lemonade sat on the patio table beside him.

"Dad, this is taking forever." Alex wiped the sweat off his forehead.

"You begged me to let you earn some extra money. Cutting the lawn is a good way to earn extra money. That's why I let you start this lawn care business."

"But this yard'll take all year to mow!"

"You've only been working ten minutes. Gotta stick with a job, even if it's hard to do. Somebody else who hires you won't be as easy on you as I am." He grinned and raised his lemonade glass.

Alex rolled his eyes. His father was always on him about being committed to whatever he did. *So that's what this is all about,* he grumbled to himself. With a sigh, he turned back to mowing.

Your Turn

1. What do you think it takes to stay committed to something?
2. Why is commitment important?
3. What do you do to "stick with a job" as Alex's father mentioned?

_____

_____

_____

_____

_____

Prayer

Lord, commitment takes hard work. Show me how to stay committed to whatever I do. Amen.

STICK WITH THIS!

Practice commitment by playing the game below. You can play by yourself or with a friend. You don't have to worry about traveling in light years. All you need to know are the multiplication facts for 4. If you come to a number that can't be divided evenly by 4 (that means NO remainder), you must say the word SPACE or go back to Earth and start over. If you make it back to Earth without taking any penalty moves, you're a "winner" even though you're playing by yourself. If you play with a friend, flip a coin to see who goes first.

COMMITMENT

God wants me to be committed to Him,
even if others are not committed.
Always give yourselves fully to the work of the Lord,
because you know that your labor in the Lord is not in vain.
1 Corinthians 15:58

Stan's Choice

Stan went to hang out with his friends at the covered bridge. Many of the kids around the apartment complex hung out there. They all went to the same middle school.

"Yeah, she acts like she's a holy roller," Babette was saying when Stan walked up.

Stan felt his blood freeze. "Who?" he asked.

"Jennifer," Steve, who lived in Stan's building said. Jennifer was a girl at Stan's church. In fact, Babette also went to Stan's church.

"Why do you say that?" Stan asked.

"She's always talking about God. I mean enough is enough, right?"

"Yeah," Steve agreed. "I go to church sometimes, but it's not my whole life."

Stan didn't agree with that. At first he wasn't going to say anything. *Maybe I should change the subject,* he thought. But he felt that God wouldn't be pleased by that. "I...believe in God like Jennifer does," he said. "I know that's what God wants."

He instantly felt embarrassed as Steve and Babette stared at him.

"Well...that's...cool," Babette said. She changed the subject after that.

Your Turn

1. How did Stan show his commitment to God?
2. What are some things that could keep you from staying committed to Jesus?

_____

_____

_____

_____

Prayer

Lord, I want to stay committed to You. I know I can with Your help. Amen.

GO THE DISTANCE

A runner who isn't committed to finishing a race will never make it to the finish line. You can decide whether you'll go the distance in your relationship with Jesus. Read Paul's pledge of commitment. What's your pledge? Write it on the trophy below.

FORGETTING WHAT IS BEHIND AND STRAINING TOWARD WHAT IS AHEAD, I PRESS ON TOWARD THE GOAL TO WIN THE PRIZE FOR WHICH GOD HAS CALLED ME HEAVENWARD IN CHRIST JESUS.

PHILIPPIANS 3:13-14

PAUL'S PLEDGE

YOUR PLEDGE

PERSEVERANCE

God wants me to persevere at hard tasks.
*Pursue a godly life, along with faith, love,
perseverance, and gentleness.*

1 Timothy 6:11, NLT

Throwing a Curve

"I'll never understand this!" Mort tossed down his glove.

"There's nothing to throwing a curve ball," his younger sister Yasmine said.

"Go away!" He hated to admit that his nine-year-old sister was probably better at pitching than he was. It wasn't that he wasn't athletic. Yasmine was just a natural at pitching.

Mort decided to go away himself — back into the house. He was glad to see that his uncle was still there.

"Keep at it, Mort," Uncle James said, after Mort explained his problem. "That's the only way you'll get better."

"Yeah." Mort didn't sound like he agreed with that.

"How badly do you want to know how to throw a curve ball?"

"Really bad," Mort said.

"If you want something badly enough, you'll keep at it."

Mort sighed. "But I keep getting it wrong!"

"That's what perseverance is all about."

Your Turn

1. Perseverance means taking commitment to a task. For what hard task do you need perseverance?
2. What tempts you to quit the most? What can you do to get past that temptation?
3. Name something you persevered at doing. What kept you going?

_____

_____

_____

Prayer

Jesus, help me to persevere at _____. I'm counting on You. Amen.

MARATHON MEN

The writer of Hebrews included a verse that shows what perseverance is all about: "Let us throw off everything that hinders and the sin that so easily entangles, and let us run with perseverance the race marked out for us. Let us fix our eyes on Jesus, the author and perfecter of our faith" (Hebrews 12:1-2). Hebrews 11 mentions some people who were models of faith and perseverance. See if you can identify who's who by marking who should receive the following awards and the details of that person's perseverance. The answers are on page 245.

He kept on building, even though others thought he was crazy. But God knew that he wasn't.

He returned to the king time and time again, even though the king kept saying, "No."

The Golden Hammer Award
Contestants
Solomon, Noah, David
What did he build?

The Try, Try Again Award
Contestants
Moses, Nehemiah
What was he after?

_____   _____

_____   _____

What award would you win for your perseverance? Why?

_____

_____

PERSEVERANCE

Persevering produces character.
We know that suffering produces perseverance; perseverance,
character; and character, hope.

Romans 5:3-4

Most Persistent

"And the award for the Most Persistent goes to Lynnleigh Saunders! The crowd goes wild!" Lynnleigh took a bow, her hairbrush/microphone held high.

"What on earth's your problem?" her twin brother, Lyle, asked.

"Why are you barging into my room?" Lynnleigh asked.

"Why are you talking to your hairbrush?" He stopped himself before he called her by the usual "doofus."

"Because I did it, Big Head!" Lynnleigh couldn't stop herself from calling him by his usual name.

"No name calling!" their mother suddenly yelled from somewhere else in the house.

Lynnleigh continued. "Remember how I talked to Laura, the new girl in the neighborhood, about God two months ago and she acted like she didn't wanna hear it?"

"Yeah. She made fun of you 'cause you asked her to come to church."

"Yeah. Well, I kept trying to be her friend. Today, she said she'd come to church this Sunday. Isn't that cool?" She and Lyle exchanged high fives.

"Y'know," Lyle said, "sometimes you're not as crazy as I think you are."

Your Turn

1. Have you ever failed at doing something you knew was right? What made you try again?

_____

2. When it comes to doing what's right, how many times are you willing to try again? (Circle one below.)

1 time   3 times   More than 5 times   As many times as it takes

Prayer

Lord, I want to have what it takes to persevere. Please give me what I need. Amen.

WHEN THE GOING GETS TOUGH...

...the tough keep on going, even if they have to suffer to do so. Fill in the crossword puzzle to find out who persevered when the going got tough. The answer is on page 245.

Across

1. Though she and her husband Aquila were forced to leave Rome, this person did not stop teaching about Christ (Acts 18:2-4).
4. He had to keep going to rebuild the wall of the city of Jerusalem.
6. A ruthless queen wanted him dead, but this prophet showed that it was hard to keep a good man of God down (1 Kings 19).
8. This woman persevered in prayer, even though the priest thought she was drunk (1 Samuel 1).

Down

1. He denied knowing Jesus three times. But he persevered. One day he preached a sermon in which 3,000 came to know Jesus (Matthew 26:69-75; Acts 2:14, 41).
2. Even after being beaten and thrown in prison, this man sang hymns with Paul to show his perseverance (Acts 16:23-25).
3. Although he was chased by Saul, who threatened his life, this man kept on going (2 Samuel 22–24).
5. He modeled perseverance by suffering and going to the cross for us.
7. This blind man persisted in calling for Jesus to heal him, even though the crowd told him to be quiet (Luke 18:35-43).

REVERENCE

God wants me to learn to respect Him.
*Men, women and children...can listen [to the Word]
and learn to fear the Lord your God and follow carefully
all the words of this law.*
Deuteronomy 31:12

Show Some Respect

Wyatt snorted with laughter from the back pew. A few heads turned in his direction, but he was having too much fun with his friends to really care.

After the church service was over, Wyatt's older brother David came looking for him. "I heard you've been clowning," he said.

"Who said that?" Wyatt asked.

"Doesn't matter. You need to cool it,when you're in church, little bro'."

"I can't talk to my friends? You used to sit back there all the time, Mom said."

"That's until I found out I wasn't showing respect for God by disturbing others who were trying to worship."

As they went to the car, Wyatt felt a little ashamed, but didn't want to admit it. He didn't think he was not respecting God by his actions. He just hadn't thought about God.

David's changed, he thought. Ever since he went to college three months earlier, David had been different somehow. He talked about God more. Wyatt glanced at his brother. David was still the coolest person he knew. Maybe there was something to what he said.

Your Turn

1. Reverence means respect. Why do you think that is important in worship?
2. How do you show reverence for God?

_____

_____

_____

Prayer

Lord, You are awesome. Amen.

REVERENCE ACROSTIC

To remind yourself that reverence for God is right, fill in the acrostic. Use words that begin with each letter to explain how you feel about God.

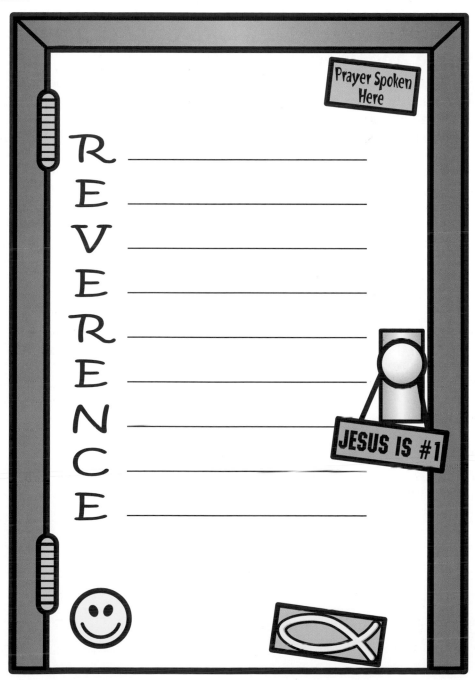

REVERENCE

Respect for God is right.
The fear of the Lord is the beginning of knowledge.

Proverbs 1:7

Where Angels Fear to Tread

"Why do you always have to do that?" Gwen asked, as she poked her head in her brother's room.

"Do what?" Scottie looked at her puzzled.

"Misusing God's name like that just because your friends do." Gwen folded her arms. "My friends and I heard you at the mall today. Every time your friends are around, you do that."

Scottie waved her away. "You're just mad because you're not cool."

"At least I know one thing you don't: disrespect for God's name isn't cool. And that makes you not cool." Gwen went off to her room. Scottie threw a pillow after her, which landed harmlessly on the floor.

What does she know? he thought. He hadn't meant anything by what he said. *God doesn't care about stuff like that, does He?* he thought. Suddenly, he wasn't so sure about that.

Your Turn

1. Do you think God cares or doesn't care about the way His name is used? If you're not sure, read Exodus 20:7.
2. What would you do if you heard a friend say something bad about God?

_____

_____

_____

_____

_____

_____

_____

Prayer

God, I want to respect You. Please show me how. Amen.

TAKE HIM SERIOUSLY

During Old Testament times, two of Moses' nephews — Nadab and Abihu — "offered unauthorized fire before the Lord" (Leviticus 10:1). Because of their failure to take the Lord seriously, they lost their lives. God wants to be taken seriously. Want to know a way to take Him very seriously? Figure out the rebus and you'll find out. Some words are sound alikes. The answers are on page 245.

TRUST

I can trust God completely.
Though you do not see him [God], *you trust him.*
1 Peter 1:8 NLT

Complete Trust

I've trotted 10 miles. I've sweat 5 gallons.

These thoughts kept bouncing around in Kyle's brain as he went up and down the sidewalk, back and forth.

Kyle's hair was sweaty, his shirt was sticking to his back and his arms felt like lead weights. Teaching a 5-year-old to ride a bike was not easy!

"Hold on tight, Kyle," Evan yelled. "I'm going to fall!"

"No way," encouraged Kyle. "Sit straight and pedal fast so you won't wobble so much." Kyle remembered his first bike ride when he was 5.

Evan's short legs pumped up and down while Kyle's long legs ran alongside his brother's bike. He steadied the bike by holding the handlebars and the back of the seat. When the bike was going in a straight line, Kyle slowly let go of the handlebars.

When Evan saw only his hands on the handlebars, he panicked. "No, Kyle!" he yelled. "Hold on! I'm gonna fall!"

"You're doing great," Kyle said. "Trust me, I won't let you fall. But...let's rest a minute."

Kyle's and Evan's mom had been watching. She brought out some lemonade and they all sat under a tree to cool off.

"Hey, Mom, I can almost ride. Kyle helped me and he won't let me fall, ever. Did you see me go?" asked Evan.

"You're doing super, Evan. And Kyle, thanks a lot for helping him. He trusts you completely. Evan knows you'll hold him up," said their mom.

Kyle gave Evan a high-five and said, "Way to go, kid."

Your Turn

1. Whom do you trust? Why?
2. What can you trust God to do for you?
3. Think of a time when you completely trusted God. What happened?

Prayer

Dear God, thank You for always keeping Your promises. Help me to always trust You in every situation. Amen.

TRUST IN GOD

A Bible verse about trust is hidden in this puzzle. To find the verse, skip every other letter in two trips around the circle. Print the letters on the blanks inside the circle. The answer is on page 245.

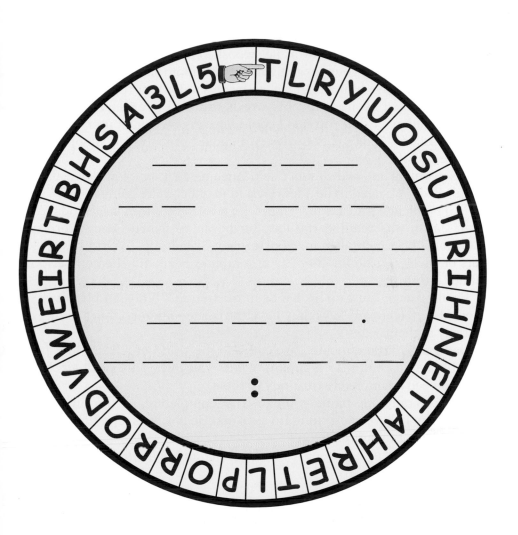

TRUST

Although people may let me down, I can always trust God.
We trust in the name of the Lord our God.

Psalm 20:7

Whom Can I Trust?

"The great day has finally arrived. I am now a very mature 12-year-old!" Jason announced dramatically as he swooshed into the kitchen.

"Happy birthday, your royal highness," his mom said.

Jason's dad gave him a high five as Jason sat down at the table.

Jason was so excited that his words tumbled over each other as he talked. "Remember that you said I could have my own computer when I was 12?" he asked. "Today is Saturday. We should probably go shopping right after breakfast!"

Jason's mom and dad couldn't help laughing. "Whoa! Slow down, Jason," said his dad. "We need to decide which kind of PC we're going to buy."

"No problem!" said Jason. "I'll get the ads I saved from last Sunday."

As Jason was reading the ads, he began to frown. They were very confusing. "Best computer for your money," read one. "Voted best PC by users of all ages," said another. "Our computer beats out the competition," claimed a third ad.

Finally Jason threw up his hands in frustration. "Who can I believe?" he asked. "Every company says they have the best computer. I don't think I can trust any of them."

Dad gave a little chuckle. "Welcome to the world of advertising, Jason. Each big name computer company wants you to buy its product. You're right, you can't completely trust any of them.

"There's only one name you can trust completely, all the time. That's God. We can believe everything He says and He always keeps His promises. I'm sure glad of that, aren't you?"

Jason nodded as he tossed aside the paper and dug into his breakfast.

Your Turn

1. What are some things or people you find hard to trust?
2. Why can you trust God?

_____

_____

Prayer

God, I trust You in every situation no matter how scary or uncertain it might be. Thanks for being completely trustworthy. Amen.

TRUST GOD

God is completely trustworthy. Use each letter in the acrostic below to name some of the things for which you trust God. For example, next to the T you might write "Takes care of me."

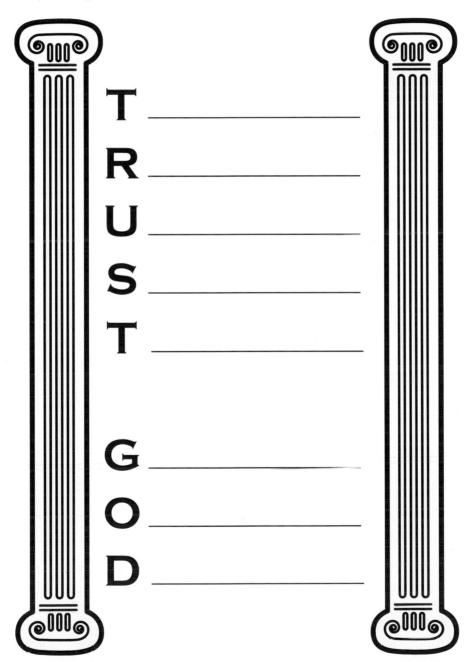

T _____

R _____

U _____

S _____

T _____

G _____

O _____

D _____

LOYALTY

God wants me to show loyalty to others.
*A friend is always loyal, and a brother is
born to help in time of need.*

Proverbs 17:17 NLT

Escaping Russell

Gotta sneak out before Russell sees me, Glenn thought as he crept to the back door. He almost had the door open when...

"Where ya going?" Russell suddenly asked.

Glenn sighed, not wanting to tell Russell that

(a) he was going out to play basketball with his friends and

(b) he didn't want his cousin Russell to go because

(c) Russell was a little...geeky.

It's not that Glenn disliked Russell. He liked him a lot. He was not only a cousin, he was also a friend. But, well, Russell just acted so...uncool sometimes. He told the worst jokes and even laughed at them when nobody else did.

"I get it," Russell said suddenly. "You don't want me to go."

Glenn felt bad. His cousin had come over just to hang out with him. And now he was trying to ditch him. He would make it up to him when he got back.

Your Turn

1. How do you think Russell felt when he learned that Glenn didn't want him to go with him? How would you feel?
2. Would you call Glenn a loyal friend? Why or why not?
3. How do you show loyalty to your friends?

_____

_____

_____

_____

_____

Prayer

Lord, thank You for the friends You have given me. Help me to be loyal to them. Amen.

GUESS WHO?

You've got three guesses to discover the identity of each loyal person described below. If you can guess correctly with the first clue, give yourself the amount of points listed. The points go down as you keep guessing. The answers are on page 245.

1.

This person wouldn't go back, even though she was told to do so.   **50 points**

This person was from Moab.   **25 points**

She wouldn't leave her mother-in-law.   **10 points**

2.

This person was the best friend a guy could have.   **50 points**

This person gave the shirt off his back, literally.   **25 points**

He was the son of Saul.   **10 points**

3.

This person had three close friends.   50 points

This person told one friend not to worry.   25 points

He raised another friend from the dead.   10 points

LOYALTY

Loyalty to God is more important than loyalty to others.
*O Lord, God of our fathers Abraham, Isaac and
Israel, keep this desire in the hearts of your people forever,
and keep their hearts loyal to you.*

1 Chronicles 29:18

Erin's Dilemma

Rasheem's Sunday school class was in the middle of their favorite game: Suppose. "Suppose your best friend didn't believe in God and expected you to do something wrong. Would you go along with your friend?" Mr. Green, the teacher, asked.

"I wouldn't," Rasheem said immediately.

"Me neither," his cousin Erin said. She didn't sound that convincing.

"You would!" Rasheem hissed. "Remember what your friend Laura wanted you to do?"

Mr. Green overheard that. "What's this?"

Erin shot Rasheem a look. She didn't want to discuss her life in front of the whole fifth and sixth grade class. While she hesitated, Rasheem said, "Laura wanted her to play this video game that my aunt didn't want Erin to play."

"I didn't want to play it either!" Erin said. "It's got occult stuff in it. Laura said she didn't see anything wrong with playing it. She said it was more interesting than church."

Some of the other kids began to talk at once. Mr. Green called for quiet. "As we were saying earlier, God wants us to be loyal to Him. If you had to choose between staying loyal to Him and being loyal to a friend, which would you choose?"

Your Turn

1. The question Mr. Green asked is for you. Which would you choose? Why?
2. How do you show loyalty to God?
3. Would God call you a loyal friend? Why or why not?

Prayer

Lord, I want to be a loyal friend to You. I need Your help. Amen.

LOYALTY RIDDLE

Time to solve another riddle. There are a number of clues you have to solve first, before you can get the answer. (Hint: Part of the answer is the name of a woman in the Bible.) The answer is on page 246.

1. This disciple of Jesus walked on water.

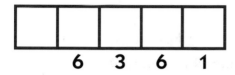

6   3   6   1

2. Mary's loyal husband.

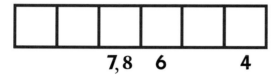

7, 8   6   4

3. Abraham was loyal to this nephew.

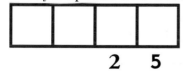

5   3

4. The loyal apostle who wrote most of the New Testament.

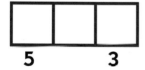

2   5

How would you describe a friend who isn't loyal?

1   2   3   4   5   6   7   8

GENEROSITY

God wants me to be a willing giver.
God loves a cheerful giver.

2 Corinthians 9:7

A Cheerful Giver

"Clarence."

Clarence looked up as his stepmother entered his room.

Mrs. Weaver sighed. "I know you think I force you to give money in church every week."

Clarence didn't say anything.

"I just wanted you to see how important it is to give. God has given us so much and..." Mrs. Weaver stopped herself. "Anyway, your father and I have talked it over. We've decided that being a 'cheerful' giver is more important, so..."

"So I don't have to put money in church if I don't want to?" Clarence looked hopeful.

"Starting next month when you turn 13." Mrs. Weaver didn't look happy about her decision.

Clarence felt like jumping for joy at first. No more giving! When his mother died, she had left him some money — money that sat in the bank now. His father gave him some of it as an allowance. His stepmother was always on him to give some of it to the offering at church.

No more giving. Suddenly, he didn't feel all that great. "Thanks," he decided. "I think...maybe I'll still give."

Your Turn

1. If you were given a choice like Clarence, would you stop giving? Why or why not?
2. Why do you think God "loves a cheerful giver"?
3. Are you a cheerful giver? How do your actions show this?

_____

_____

_____

Prayer

Help me Lord to be a cheerful giver. Amen.

GENEROUS TO A FAULT?

Welcome to "Get the Facts," the show the helps you get the facts. Today, we'll look at Ananias and Sapphira, a generous couple who gave money to help the Christians in their community. But were they really as generous as they claimed to be? Use the code to get the facts on this couple from Acts 5:1-11. The answer is on page 245.

Ananias and Sapphira sold some ⬛⬛⬛ _____ and gave

the money to the apostles. Ananias and his wife kept part of the money

but still claimed that they gave all that they had received. But Peter knew

that Ananias had ⬛⬛⬛⬛ _____ to the Holy Spirit about the

amount of money he had received for the ⬛⬛⬛ _____.

Because of that, Ananias ⬛⬛⬛ _____ instantly!

When his wife arrived, she was asked how much money they received.

She gave the same answer that her husband did. Because of that, she

⬛⬛⬛ _____ too! Everyone was terrified!

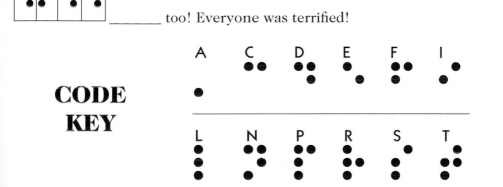

CODE KEY

A	C	D	E	F	I

L	N	P	R	S	T

GENEROSITY

Generous giving inspires generosity in return.
*A farmer who plants only a few seeds will get a small crop. But
the one who plants generously will get a generous crop.*

2 Corinthians 9:6, NLT

The Gift

"Oh, I'm so embarrassed! I can't believe I don't have another dollar."

Ben Adams felt sorry as he heard the woman ahead of him in line. He glanced at his mother, who looked annoyed. Other people in line were starting to grumble. Finally, Ben reached into his pocket. "Here," he said, as he gave the woman a dollar.

"I can't take…" the woman began.

"That's okay," Ben said.

"Is this your son?" the woman asked Mrs. Adams. "You should be proud of him."

"Always am," Mrs. Adams said.

The woman asked for their names and address to return the dollar, but Ben didn't think he'd ever see that dollar again.

"That was a very nice thing to do," his mother said as they were on their way to the car.

Ben shrugged, but he was pleased at her praise. He knew he had done something God wanted him to do.

A few days later, a package came for him in the mail. Inside was a five-dollar bill, a video game cartridge, and a note: "Thank you for your generosity. I was almost late getting to a meeting. Thanks to you, I made it in time. My company makes these games. Hope you like this one."

Ben stared at his mother, speechless.

Your Turn

1. Have you ever given a gift and received one in return? How did that make you feel?

2. Do you think people should give in order to receive something back? Why or why not?

Prayer

Lord, I want to give, not to always receive something back, but because giving pleases You. Amen.

YOUR GIVING

Giving does not always mean money. You can give your time or use your talents to help someone. You just have to know what the needs are. Fill in what you know about the needs in your area. What can you do to meet those needs? Don't forget to ask God how you can help.

What are some needs you know of in your...

home?

_____

_____

_____

church?

_____

_____

_____

neighborhood?

_____

_____

_____

Your talents and abilities:

_____

_____

_____

PATIENCE

God supplies all of my needs in His time.
If we hope for what we do not yet have, we wait for it patiently.
Romans 8:25

Model Building

Casey was waiting in the car for his 17-year-old brother, Eric. Eric was driving Casey to the hobby shop downtown. Casey leaned over and blasted the horn just as Eric came out of the house.

"Knock it off!" Eric said as he got into the car. "What's the big rush?"

"Well, they have this really cool model of a 1957 Corvette on sale. I want to hurry and get one before they're all sold out," Casey answered.

"That is a neat model," Eric agreed. "But it has hundreds of pieces. Sure you're ready for that?"

Later when Casey opened the box, he understood what Eric was talking about. Instead of hundreds of pieces, it looked like zillions! And the directions were 10 pages long! He started sorting pieces and gluing them together. After two hours, it looked as though he had hardly done anything. *This is taking too long,* Casey thought. *I'll take some shortcuts. I don't need to do all these steps.*

"How's the model coming?" Eric asked later, as he came into the room.

"Not so good," mumbled Casey. "I worked four hours and hardly anything is done. And it doesn't look right."

Eric asked, "Did you follow the directions, step by step?"

"Well, most of them," Casey said.

"You have to work carefully and follow every direction when you build a model," said Eric. "When you skip directions, you can end up in a mess."

"It takes so long to do all that sanding, fitting and gluing," Casey said.

"To build models, you need to be very patient. It's not something that's done in a hurry. When it's finally finished, you can really be proud of it." said Eric.

This will be a masterpiece, even if it takes all winter, thought Casey as he carefully unglued a piece that was in the wrong place.

Your Turn

1. What makes you impatient?
2. What are some of the things that can happen when you're impatient?

_____

_____

Prayer

Thanks for being patient with me. Help me to learn to wait for things. Amen.

PATIENCE OF JOB

An Old Testament believer, Job, is often called a patient man. When everything in his life went wrong, he wanted to talk to God. Instead, God asked Job some questions to help him understand that God takes care of everything in His time. Fill in the blanks, using verses from Job 39 in an NIV Bible. The answers are on page 246.

Do you know when the mountain _____ give birth?

Who let the wild _____ go free?

Will the wild _____ consent to serve you?

The wings of the _____ flap joyfully, but they cannot compare with the feathers of the _____.

Do you give the _____ his strength?

Does the _____ soar at your command?

Does the _____ take flight by your wisdom?

PATIENCE

I can show God's love by being patient.
Love is patient, love is kind.

1 Corinthians 13:4

Blast Off!

Twelve-year-old Jeff Wilkens jumped out of bed, hopped into his clothes and rushed into the kitchen. He gulped down some juice and a bowl of cereal, then bolted out to the garage. His brother Andrew was home from college for the weekend. They were going to put the finishing touches on a remote control rocket they had built.

When Jeff opened the garage door he was annoyed to find their younger brother, Pete, with Andrew. "Hey, man," Andrew called. "Let's get this finished and on the launch pad."

"Hooray!" yelled Pete as he shoved a stool into place.

Everything they needed was spread out on the workbench.

Jeff tightened two screws. Ver-r-ry slowly Pete turned the third screw. "Hurry up! We need to finish this," said Jeff.

Then Jeff started putting on the decals. Pete held a decal in his hand, trying to decide where to stick it. Jeff reached for the decal. "Let me do it! You're slower than a turtle," he snapped at Pete.

"I quit," Pete said and wiped his eyes.

"Time out," Andrew said from the other side of the garage. "Jeff, we have all day to finish this rocket. There's no big rush. You have to remember that you're five years older than Pete. He can't do things as quickly as you can. You need to be patient."

Jeff knew Andrew was right. He gave Pete a friendly poke, "Hey, little bro. I'm sorry. Take as long as you want. And you can push the button for the first launch."

"All right!" Pete yelled as he high-fived his big brothers.

Your Turn

1. What things make you impatient?
2. What do you do when you lose your patience?

Prayer

Heavenly Father, help me to be more patient with people and things that concern me. Amen.

PATIENCE, PATIENCE

How much patience would you have in these situations? Check the patience level that fits. It may take patience to do this activity!

	Lots	Some	Little	None
Waiting for your turn in a game.				
Waiting for something you really want.				
Waiting in the dentist's or doctor's office.				
Waiting for your parents to decide if you can go somewhere with your friends.				
Waiting for your little brother or sister.				
Waiting for a big math test.				
Waiting for a special trip or holiday.				
Waiting to use the telephone.				
Waiting for dinner.				
Waiting to mow the lawn.				
Waiting to find out if you made the team.				

GOODNESS

True goodness comes from God.
*Make every effort to add to your faith goodness;
and to goodness, knowledge.*

2 Peter 1:5

True Goodness

"Can I get this one, Mom?" Eric Nielson held up a CD.

His mother quickly read the CD's song list. " 'It's Fun to Be Wicked'?" she read aloud. "And this is by…The Evil Trolls?! I don't think so, Eric."

"But everybody's listening to this."

"It's got a parent advisory sticker on it. Besides, there's nothing 'fun' about evil. Why don't these groups sing about being good?"

Eric made a face. Whenever he heard the word good, he thought of his cousin Michael. Michael always tried to be good, even though he was a big sneak. Everyone in the family talked about how good Michael was.

"I know that look. What's up?"

"Michael."

Mrs. Nielson smiled. "I know you think everybody but you is fooled by Michael's behavior. Michael tries to be good, but I know that's just an act. True goodness comes from God. It's a kindness that comes from the heart. You don't have to try to be good. You just are."

Your Turn

1. Do you know someone like Michael? If so, how do you react to his or her attempts to be "good"?
2. Do you ever "try" to be good? What happens as a result?
3. Goodness is a fruit of the Holy Spirit. Why do you think this quality is important?

_____

_____

_____

_____

Prayer

Lord, let the fruit of goodness grow and ripen in my life. Amen.

GOOD OR JUST GOOD-LOOKING?

A professional ballplayer's statistics show whether he or she is good. True goodness is also shown by a person's "statistics": his or her actions. Look at the two men below. Are they good or just good-looking? You decide. Read the Scripture listed. Check off the box beside your vote. Give a reason why you voted the way that you did.

Saul
First King of Israel
Stats:
- 1 Samuel 9:1
- 1 Samuel 15:1-3
- 1 Samuel 15:9
- 1 Samuel 15:24

❏ Good

❏ Just good-looking?

Why?

_____

_____

David
A shepherd
(soon to be king of Israel)
Stats:
- 1 Samuel 16:11-12
- Acts 13:22

❏ Good

❏ Just good-looking?

Why?

_____

_____

GOODNESS

Jesus' goodness helps me be good toward others.
I will see the goodness of the Lord in the land of the living.
Psalm 27:13

Try, Try, Again?

"Dad, I'm so sick of trying to be good all the time!" Max Fielding said as he flopped on a chair in his father's office.

"You mean you want to start teasing your sister again?" Mr. Fielding eyed him from behind his computer.

"I can't help it, Dad."

"I heard that!" his sister yelled from the family room.

"You don't have to try, Max."

"I don't?! Cool!" Max jumped up and started off toward the family room.

"Whoa! You believe that Jesus died for your sins, right?"

Max was thrown for a minute. What did that have to do with the fact that he was now free to tease his sister? "Yeah," he said wondering where this conversation was going.

"So, that means we don't have to try to be good. Because Jesus is the only one who was ever really good, His goodness helps us to treat others fairly. That's what I meant when I said you didn't have to try."

Max looked disappointed, which made his father laugh.

Your Turn

1. Have you ever felt frustrated at trying to be "good"? What did you do?
2. If you know that you can't be good all the time on your own, does that mean you don't have to try at all? Why or why not?

_____

_____

_____

_____

_____

Prayer

Lord, with Your help, I can live a life that is pleasing to you. Amen.

WHERE GOODNESS CAN BE FOUND

Shade in the areas below that contain a number that can be divided equally by 7. You'll find the last place on earth where a person would expect goodness to be found. Yet in this place, it was there in abundance. The answer is on page 246.

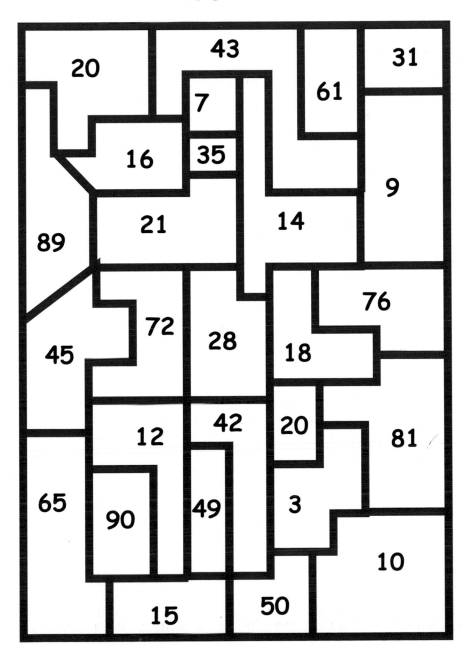

WISDOM

I can ask God for wisdom.
*If you want to know what God wants you to do,
ask him, and he will gladly tell you.*

James 1:5a, LB

A Wise Move

"How do you know what to do?" Devin asked his friend Jeff. The boys were at Jeff's house playing computer games.

"I already told you to hit the key button to get out of that maze." Jeff pointed to the computer screen.

"I'm not talking about this." Devin paused the game. "How do you know...y'know, what's the right thing to do and stuff?"

Jeff knew that Devin wasn't a Christian. Devin was curious about God and about Jeff's church. He usually asked Jeff lots of questions.

"My dad says you can ask God to help you know what to do. Knowing to ask God for help is the beginning of wisdom." Jeff grinned. "Just like you knew to ask for my help 'cause I'm so much better than you at this game. That was smart."

"Yeah, right. Then how come I'm beating your score?"

Jeff tried to wrestle the joystick away from Devin.

Your Turn

1. When you're not sure what to do about a problem, where do you go for advice?
2. Does wisdom mean the same as being smart? Why or why not?
3. For what do you need wisdom? Use the prayer below.

_____

_____

_____

_____

_____

Prayer

Lord, I'm asking you for wisdom to _____ (fill in the blank). Amen.

ANOTHER WISE MOVE

Solve each rebus for wise advice. Some words are sound-alikes. The answer is on page 246.

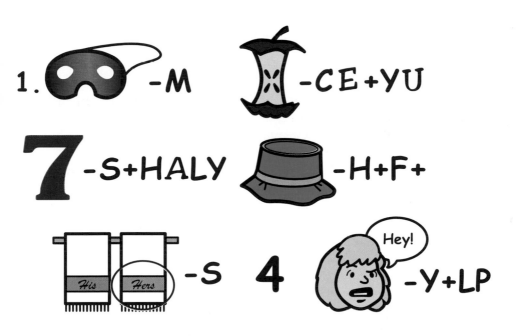

WISDOM

God's Word helps me on the road to wisdom.
*God's laws are perfect. They protect us, make us wise,
and give us joy and light.*

Psalm 19:7-8 LB

Great-Grandfather

"Your great-grandfather must be, like, two million years old," Richard whispered.

"Well, he is old," Chan whispered back. "I'm not sure how old he is. My mom says he's pretty smart. He used to teach tae kwon do."

"Cool."

"I haven't lost my hearing," Chan's great-grandfather said, followed by a chuckle. "I'm 83. Want to know a secret, something I learned when I was a boy in Korea a long time ago?"

Richard and Chan looked at each other and shrugged. "Yeah, okay," Chan said.

"God's Word can help you be wise."

Richard looked disappointed. He had hoped Chan's great-grandfather knew something about being a ninja or something.

"That's good advice, young man," Great-grandfather said, "even if you don't think so right now."

Richard looked embarrassed. Chan grinned. "Told ya' he was smart," Chan said.

Your Turn

1. What was Chan's great-grandfather's advice? Why would this advice be helpful?
2. Think of a time when something in God's Word helped you make a right decision. If a friend needed some advice, what would you tell him or her about God's Word?

_____

_____

_____

Prayer

Lord Jesus, thank You for Your Word. Amen.

PROBLEMS, PROBLEMS

Your job is to help the kid below to use the advice from the Word to solve the problems listed. Which verses will you choose? Write your advice below, based on the Scriptures.

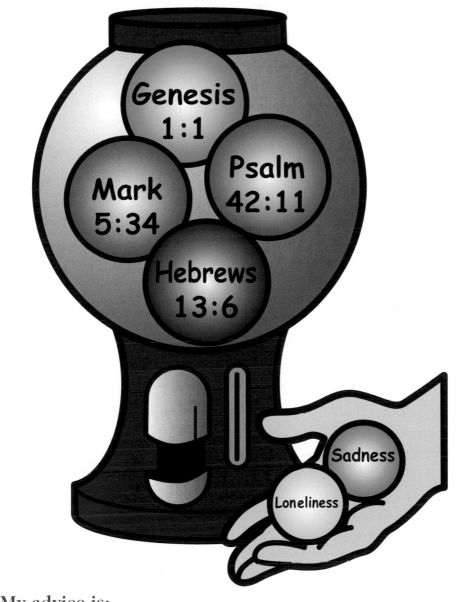

My advice is: _____

_____

_____

THANKFULNESS

A thankful attitude shows.

So then, just as you received Christ Jesus as Lord, continue to live in him...overflowing with thankfulness.

Colossians 2:6-7

The Gift

Chris reluctantly unwrapped the gift from his great aunt. She always gave him "dumb" things like sweaters and hats that she knitted. *Why can't she ever buy me something?* he wondered.

"Did you tell your aunt, 'Thank you'?" His mother frowned at him.

"Thanks," Chris mumbled. He didn't feel thankful at all.

"My pleasure," his aunt beamed.

"Chris, we need to talk about your attitude," his mother said when they drove away from the retirement center where his great aunt lived.

"Why? Mom, why should I pretend I like these things?" Chris poked at the sweater in the box on his lap.

"I'm not asking you to pretend, Chris. I just want you to realize that your aunt didn't have to give you anything for your birthday." His mother sighed. "I'm almost tempted to return this envelope." She handed Chris a worn-looking envelope. "Your aunt gave me this for you as well."

Inside was a $20 bill. "All right!" Chris said.

His mother sighed again. "Chris, we need to have a long talk about being thankful."

Your Turn

1. Was Chris thankful for his aunt's gift? Why or why not?
2. What are you most thankful for?

_____

_____

_____

_____

_____

Prayer

Lord, I want to have a thankful attitude. Amen.

YOUR PSALM OF THANKS

Psalm 66 is a psalm of thanks to God. (Take a quick look at a few verses.) Praising God is a way to thank Him. For what would you like to thank God? Use the space below to say, "Thanks." You can write a prayer or use a picture to express your thanks.

God,

THANKFULNESS

I can express my thanks for what others do for me.
Thanks be to God for his indescribable gift!
2 Corinthians 9:15

Canoe Trip

"Did you enjoy the trip?"

Kyle nodded at his stepfather's question. "This has been the best canoe trip ever!" He leaned back in his sleeping bag. He felt tired. It was a good sort of tired. They had almost capsized on the river dozens of times, but Kyle had still enjoyed the ride.

He hadn't been thrilled when his mother remarried. He knew his stepfather had tried to win him over. At first, Kyle hadn't wanted to be bothered. But the love his stepfather had for his mother and for God had slowly worked on him.

Just before he dropped off to sleep, Kyle said, "Thanks for bringing me, Dad." The "Dad" part had slipped out. Kyle had said he wouldn't ever call Dale that. This time...it felt right.

There was a long pause before his stepfather spoke again. "You're welcome, son. Thank you."

"For what?"

"For agreeing to be my son."

Your Turn

1. How did Kyle show his thanks for the trip?
2. Think of a time when you said, "Thanks" to someone. How did you express your thanks?
3. Why is it important to say thank you?

_____

_____

_____

_____

_____

Prayer

Lord, help me remember to show my thanks. Amen.

GRATITUDE ATTITUDE

It's easy to spot the kid below who has an attitude of gratitude. But some attitudes aren't so easy to spot. They're attitudes of the heart. Check out the people below. Who had an attitude of gratitude? Put a check under Column B. Who had an attitude of ingratitude? Put a check in Column A. Need help? Check the Scripture underneath each person.

Gift	Column A	Column B
1. Hannah a son (1 Samuel 1:27–2:2)		
2. Adam Eve (Genesis 2:23)		
3. Israelites freedom from slavery (Exodus 16:2-3)		
4. Jewish leaders Jesus (bread of life) (John 6:41-42)		
5. People in Iconium The Gospel message (Acts 14:3, 5)		

Think of a gift you recently received. Under which column would you fall? Why?

_____

_____

_____

HONESTY

God wants me to tell the whole truth,
not just the parts I think are best.
*You deserve honesty from the heart; yes,
utter sincerity and truthfulness.*

Psalm 51:6a, LB

The Excuse

Bernard did some fast thinking. How would he convince his grandmother that the whole thing wasn't his fault? Quinn made him mad, mad enough to cause the two of them to get into a shoving match. That had resulted in an in-school detention, which was why he was late.

I'll just tell her that I had some school work to do after school, he decided. *That's sort of true.*

Bernard couldn't look his grandmother in the eye as he explained why he was late. After he finished, she said, "Bernard, I've been your grandmother for the past 12 years."

Bernard, who was 12, agreed.

"I know when you're about to lie to me or at least not tell me the whole truth. Are you telling me the whole story?"

Bernard squirmed. "Uh…" He finally gave up and told her everything.

Grandmother shook her head. "Bernard, you know that lying's wrong. Anyway, I'm glad you told me the truth."

"How did you know that I didn't tell you everything at first?"

She smiled. "I think that will be my little secret."

Your Turn

1. Why didn't Bernard want to tell his grandmother the whole truth?
2. When are you tempted to keep back part of the truth?
3. Why is not telling the whole truth the same as lying?

_____

_____

_____

_____

Prayer

Lord, help me tell the whole truth and nothing but the truth. Amen.

SIGNS OF THE TRUTH

Ready for more semaphore? (Hey, that rhymes!) The Bible has a lot to say about being truthful. It's up to you to figure out what this verse (Leviticus 19:11) is saying. The answer is on page 246.

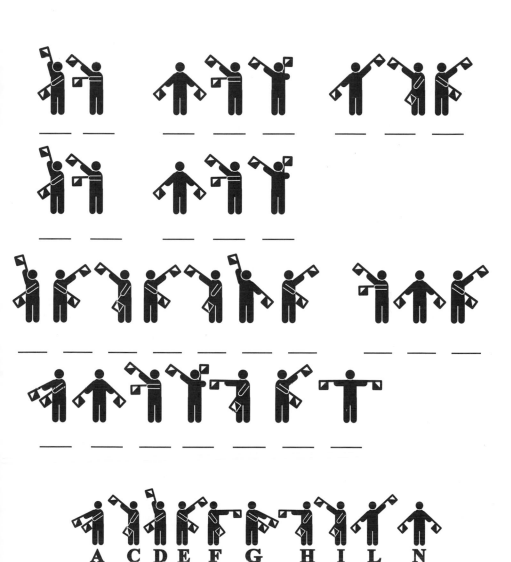

HONESTY

Honesty and grace go hand in hand.
A gentle answer turns away wrath, but a
harsh word stirs up anger.

Proverbs 15:1

To Tell the Truth

"There!" Moira held up the project she had finished in pottery class. "What do you think?"

"What is it?" her brother Steven asked.

"It's a vase!"

"If you say so."

"I'm afraid to ask what you think now."

The words "hideous," "ugly" and "you've gotta be kidding" came to his mind. Stephen felt the vase deserved one of the three. He couldn't help remembering how Moira had teased him about a drawing he had once made. But the look on Moira's face stopped him. He knew she had worked hard on that vase, even though it looked as if an elephant sat on it.

The WWJD button Moira had once given him caught his eye. What would Jesus do in this situation? "I know you worked hard on it," he said, knowing that was the truth. "Mom will appreciate it." That was also true. Their mother liked anything they gave her.

"You think so? Thanks, Steve." Moira left the room looking happy. Steven sighed with relief.

Your Turn

1. Why do you think Steven did not tell Moira exactly what he thought?
2. How can you give an honest, yet gentle answer?

_____

_____

_____

_____

Prayer

Lord, I want to be honest, but I don't want to hurt people. Help me know the difference. Amen.

A GENTLE ANSWER

Sometimes we say things we regret later. If only we could rewind the tapes of our lives! How can these kids give a better answer than the one they gave? You can hit "rewind" on the remote. With Proverbs 15:1 in mind, give your suggestion for what could be said. Use the blank speech balloons. Why is a gentle answer more helpful? Possible answers are on page 246.

FORGIVENESS

When you forgive others, God can forgive you.
Forgive and you will be forgiven.

Luke 6:37b

Unforgiven

Stuart Leonard stared at his younger brother. He knew Linus wasn't sorry. Linus always took Stuart's stuff without asking. This time, Stuart had caught him red-handed.

"Are you gonna forgive me?" Linus asked.

I'm sick of forgiving him, Stuart thought. Aloud he said, "You're not really sorry, so no."

Linus looked ready to cry. But Stuart didn't care. Linus didn't deserve to be forgiven.

Later, Mrs. Leonard called him in the living room. "Did you take one of your dad's tools without asking?" she asked.

Stuart knew that he had. "Uh, yeah."

Mrs. Leonard folded her arms. "I told you about that before."

"Sorry, Mom."

Mrs. Leonard shook her head. "Do you think you should be forgiven if you're not going to forgive your brother for the same thing?"

Stuart stared at her. *She must've heard us*, he thought. "At least I'm sorry. Linus never is."

"That still doesn't give you the right to hold a grudge, does it?"

Stuart wanted to say "Yes!" but knew that he couldn't. "I get the message."

Your Turn

1. Did Stuart have the right to not forgive his brother? Why or why not?
2. Has someone ever told you he or she would not forgive you? How did you feel?
3. Is there ever something a person could do that shouldn't be forgiven? Why or why not?

_____

_____

_____

Prayer

Lord, thank You for the forgiveness You always offer. Amen.

WHAT'S WRONG?

What's wrong with this picture? Find eight things wrong. You probably couldn't "fix" most of the things that are wrong, but there is one thing you can change to make this a "picture" of forgiveness. The answer is on page 246.

FORGIVENESS

God helps us forgive those who hurt us.

Bear with each other and forgive whatever grievances you may have against one another. Forgive as the Lord forgave you.

Colossians 3:13

Forgiveness for a Friend

"What's wrong?" Megan asked as soon as she saw her older brother Joseph.

"Nothing." Joseph threw his backpack on the kitchen table, almost knocking over the vase on top of it.

"Something's wrong. Is it about that lie Nathan told about you?" Megan explained how even the kids in her fourth grade class knew that Joseph's friend Nathan had lied to avoid getting in trouble for something he had done. The principal found out the truth and called Nathan to his office.

Joseph nodded. "Nathan told me he was sorry. But I don't know if I can forgive him for what he did."

"But Jesus said we're supposed to. If you can't, He'll help you."

Joseph stared at her. He hadn't expected such an answer to come from her.

Megan grinned. "That's what Dad just told me a few minutes ago when I told him I didn't want to forgive you for making fun of my dress the other day. If I can forgive you, can you forgive Nathan?"

Your Turn

1. Why do you think Joseph had a hard time forgiving Nathan?
2. When have you found it difficult to forgive someone? What did you do?

_____

_____

_____

_____

_____

Prayer

Lord, thank You for the grace to forgive others. Amen.

FAMILY FORGIVENESS

Another person named Joseph was able to forgive even though his family members turned against him. Perhaps you've read about him in the Bible. If so, you know the story well enough to tell what was happening in his life, based on these images. The answers are on page 246.

1
Genesis 37:3
What's going on?

3
Genesis 45:4-8
What's going on?

2
Genesis 39:20
What's going on?

RESPONSIBILITY

God wants us to take our responsibilities seriously.
Whatever you do, work at it with all your heart, as working for the Lord, not for men.

Colossians 3:23

Being Responsible

Gordon sighed as he heard Mrs. Nakamura complaining to his father in the backyard. Mrs. Nakamura had asked his father to come over and give her bushes a trim. Gordon had begged his father to let him do it.

He didn't see what the big deal was. So he'd shown up a little late to her house. So he'd trimmed one bush until it looked like a lopsided egg. He said he'd come back and even it out after he and his friends finished playing street hockey.

His father soon came into Gordon's room. "I told you trimming bushes is a big responsibility," he said.

"What's the big deal, Dad? I told her I'd finish later." Gordon sounded huffy.

His father sighed. "The big deal is that it is a big deal if you're doing something for someone else. It's one way of showing that you're responsible. That means showing up on time, doing a good job and making sure that you complete the job. I think Mrs. Nakamura wouldn't have gotten too upset if you'd just shown up on time. That would've proved that you were serious about this."

Your Turn

1. How much responsibility did Gordon show? You decide by circling a number on the line below.

1   2   3   4   5   6   7   8   9   10
(NOT MUCH)   (A LOT)

2. When was the last time someone gave you a challenging task to handle? How seriously did you take the responsibility? Circle a response.

Pretty seriously   I'm not sure   Not seriously (Hey, I'm still learning!)

Prayer

Lord Jesus, help me to take my responsibilities seriously. Amen.

RESPONSIBILITY YOUR WAY

Take a minute to think about your responsibilities. (Chores? Getting your homework done? Taking the dog for a walk?) List what you've got to do and when it's got to be done. Put a star by the hardest task facing you. Then ask God for help to do what needs to be done.

What?...   When?...

RESPONSIBILITY

Responsibility comes when I'm ready for it.
These men were considered trustworthy. They were made
responsible for distributing the supplies to their brothers.
Nehemiah 13:13b

Who's Responsible?

Gordon knew that his parents didn't think he was too responsible. But after the talking-to he received because of the bush-trimming incident, he wanted to prove that he could be responsible. That included being able to stay at home by himself.

His parents exchanged a doubtful look.

"I'm almost 13!" Gordon yelled. "I know not to let anybody come over or to let the house burn down." He looked slightly embarrassed. "I won't let what happened last time happen."

The last time his parents had gone on a "date" as they called it, he had accidentally left the phone off the hook and was partially responsible for nearly setting fire to the kitchen table.

Anyway, hadn't he proven himself this past week that he could be responsible? He had done all of his chores, done his homework without being forced to and even returned some overdue library books!

"Okay, we're willing to trust you," Mr. Archer said. "We think you might be ready."

"Might be?" Gordon asked.

Mrs. Archer smiled. "We'll give it a trial run," she said.

Your Turn

1. How did Gordon prove that he was ready for more responsibility?
2. What big responsibilities do you think you're ready for? Why?

_____

_____

_____

_____

_____

Prayer

Lord, make me ready for more and more responsibility. Amen.

READY, WILLING AND ABLE?

People who want to find jobs or jobs with more experience usually write a resume. The resume shows their experience. Are you ready for more responsibility? How can your past experience be used to show your willingness and ability? Use the space below to list the responsibility for which you feel you're ripe. Then take an inventory of your life by listing your experience. List whatever you think will help. (For example: projects you've been involved in or chores you've done successfully without complaining.) Then list the stoppers. These are what keep you from fulfilling your responsibilities (putting things off, too busy, and so on). How can you keep the stoppers from stopping you?

Responsibility you want:

_____

_____

_____

_____

_____

Past experience:

_____

_____

_____

_____

Stoppers:

_____

_____

_____

_____

COURAGE

God gives me the courage to do what's right.
Do not be afraid; do not be discouraged.
Be strong and courageous.

Joshua 10:25

The Prank

"Did you see what happened?"

Keith wished he could suddenly fake an injury to get out of answering the assistant principal's question. But he had seen what happened. His friend Terry had set off a firecracker in the restroom that frightened someone into setting off the fire alarm.

Keith hadn't wanted to say anything, especially after the principal threatened to make all of the boys stay after school until someone finally confessed. He didn't want to get Terry in trouble. *He's caused all of us to get in trouble*, he thought. But if I tell, won't Mr. Chavez just think I had something to do with it?

He suddenly thought about prayer. His Sunday school teacher had challenged the class to keep close to God during the week through prayer.

Lord, I'm afraid. Help me do what's right, Keith prayed silently.

After another sigh, Keith finally told what he saw. He was relieved that Mr. Chavez seemed to believe him. But what was even more of a relief was when Terry himself came in to confess what he'd done.

Thanks, God, Keith prayed.

Your Turn

1. What did Keith need courage to do?
2. When have you needed courage?
3. When do you need courage the most? Use the prayer below to talk to God.

_____

_____

_____

Prayer

Dear God, I need courage to _____ . Help me do what's right. Amen.

THE RIGHT STUFF

Having "the right stuff" means having the courage and determination to do what you have to do. God gave the following people the right stuff to do what had to be done. During one period in Israel's history, God gave judges the courage to lead the Israelites against their enemies. Most of the time they were outnumbered. Match the person with a "nickname" that describes his or her task. The answer is on page 246.

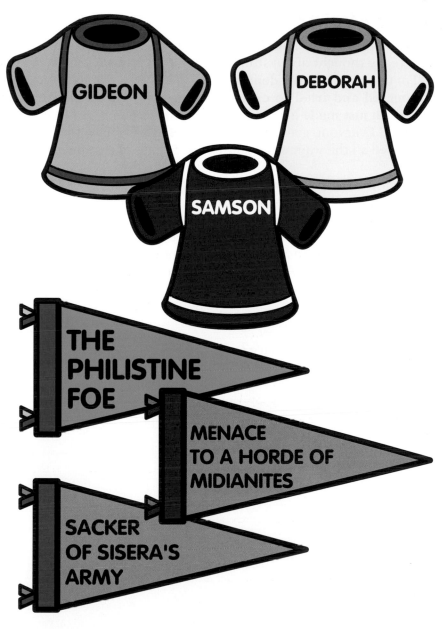

COURAGE

God gives us the courage to face our fears.
The Lord is my light and my salvation — whom shall I fear? The Lord is the stronghold of my life — of whom shall I be afraid?

Psalm 27:1

What, Me Afraid?

Fear? Chet wanted to laugh. Fear was for wusses. But he was afraid. He hadn't really thought about it until his mother had said those dreaded words: "I'm taking you to the dentist."

Chet begged and tried to excuse his way out. He'd even thrown a tantrum, which just made his mother mad. "You're going and that's that!" she declared. "Everyone goes for regular checkups."

Chet sulked all the way to the dentist. And that's when she asked, "Are you afraid?"

Chet tried to bluff his way out, but finally nodded. "I thought so," his mother continued. "Well, remember you can always ask God for courage when you're afraid. But the first thing you have to do is admit that you're afraid."

God, I'm afraid. Please help me. Chet almost felt better just thinking those words. Now if only he could get out of going to the dentist.

Your Turn

1. What was Chet's fear?
2. What fear or fears do you have?
3. How do you deal with your fears?

_____

_____

_____

_____

_____

Prayer

Lord, when I'm afraid, I'm glad I can come to You. Amen.

COURAGE COMMAND

God gives you a promise that can help you be courageous. It's found in Jeremiah 33:3. All you have to do is figure out the signs. The answer is on page 246.

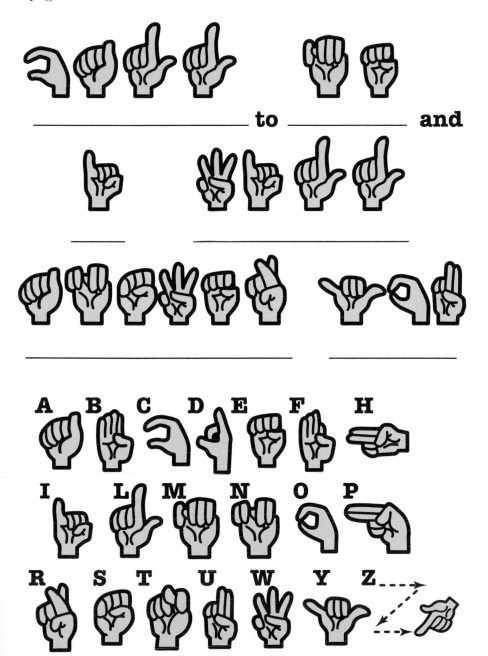

_____ to _____ and

_____   _____

A B C D E F H
I L M N O P
R S T U W Y Z

FAIRNESS

God is always fair.
*Whoever believes in him [Jesus] shall not
perish but have eternal life.*

John 3:16

It's Not Fair!

"You sure look like a black thundercloud ready to spit lightning," Grandma Rogers said to Connor. "What has you all riled up?"

Connor flopped onto the couch and said, "It's just not fair! I practiced pitching for weeks getting ready for team tryouts. But did I get that position? No! Brad Hanson got it. And he didn't even practice at all!"

Grandma listened as Connor complained. Then she said, "Once I knew a woman who had a husband and three kids. The woman was happy.

"After a while, the children grew up and moved away. Then suddenly, without any warning, her husband died of a heart attack. To make matters worse, she started to have problems herself. Her legs hurt all the time and she had trouble walking. She became very angry.

"People tried to help her but all she did was whine and complain that it just wasn't fair that she had all these problems.

"A friend told her, 'Life's not fair. But even though the world doesn't always treat us fairly, God is always fair. Think about the good things in your life that God gives you.'

"The woman kept thinking about what her friend said. Gradually she smiled more than she frowned and was positive more than complaining."

"How did the woman turn out?" asked Connor.

Grandma laughed and said, "That woman was me. What do you think?"

"I think you turned out great," Connor said. "Sorry I was such a grump."

"No offense taken," Grandma replied.

Your Turn

1. How do you react to unfairness?
2. What is the difference between fairness and justice? (Look up both words in a dictionary.)

Prayer

Almighty God, I'm happy that You're always fair. Help me to treat others fairly. Amen.

LIFE'S NOT FAIR!

The purple words in this Bible verse are hidden in the word search. They can be found across, up and down, backward, forward, and diagonally. The answers are on page 246.

I have observed something else in this world of ours. The fastest runner doesn't always win the race, and the strongest warrior doesn't always win the battle. The wise are often poor, and the skillful are not necessarily wealthy. And those who are educated don't always lead successful lives.   ~ Ecclesiastes 9:11 NLT

```
S  U  C  C  E  S  S  F  U  L  I
T  W  E  A  L  T  H  Y  U  O  N
R  O  O  P  G  O  D  F  R  B  D
O  B  E  R  E  B  L  A  O  S  E
N  A  A  S  E  L  R  S  I  E  T
G  T  W  A  I  Y  O  T  R  R  A
E  T  S  K  F  W  W  E  R  V  C
S  L  S  L  I  V  E  S  A  E  U
T  E  T  N  A  I  R  T  W  D  D
E  C  A  R  U  N  N  E  R  O  E
```

FAIRNESS

God wants me to be fair to other people.
Do to others what you would have them do to you.

Matthew 7:12

The Golden Rule

Sean had been hanging by the telephone all evening. Each time it rang, he raced to pick it up. His sister Molly began to tease him. "Sean's got a girlfriend," she said in a sing-song voice.

"I do not! Get out of here, Molly!" Sean yelled.

The yelling brought their mom into the room. "What's going on here?" she demanded. Sean and Molly told their sides and declared a truce.

After Molly left, Sean's mom said, "Obviously, you're expecting a call. Want to tell me about it?"

"Oh, it's just that stupid Marc," Sean said.

Mom looked surprised, "I thought Marc was your best friend."

"Sure, ever since first grade. But not anymore. Today he didn't choose me to be his partner in science class. Instead, he chose the new kid, Chad." Sean looked at his feet and let out a big sigh. "He even laughed when I tripped in the library and dropped my books. I've been sitting by the phone all night because Marc was supposed to call about going to the hobby show this weekend. It's just not fair. Marc and I always did everything together. Well, I'll show him. I won't invite him to go camping with us. Then see how he feels!"

"Whoa! Stop right there," his mom said. "Now you're being unfair. I think you need to learn the Golden Rule."

"What's that?"

"It's something Jesus said," Mrs. O'Gara explained. "We are to treat others the way we want to be treated. I don't think you'd want Marc to leave you out of the camping trip."

"No, guess not," Sean admitted. "And I probably did look pretty silly with my books flying all over."

Your Turn

1. Was Marc being unfair to Sean? Why or why not?
2. How can you follow the Golden Rule?

_____

_____

Prayer

God, help me remember the Golden Rule and live by it. Amen.

FOLLOW THE RULE

Rank these things according to their unfairness from 1-6, with 6 being the most unfair. Then write something below the chart from your own life that seems unfair. How can you honor God and follow the Golden Rule in all of these situations?

	1	2	3	4	5	6
Christians get bad diseases or are in accidents.						
Your best friend ignores you.						
You study really hard and still get a bad grade on a test.						
Innocent people get killed in a war.						
Your parents won't allow you to watch certain TV shows or videos.						
Your Dad's company is moving and your family has to move across country.						
Your older brother or sister gets more privileges than you do.						

FAITH

Faith is believing without seeing.
*Faith is being sure of what we hope for and
certain of what we do not see.*

Hebrews 11:1

Faith Test

Garrett tested the ice with one foot. He wasn't quite sure the pond was completely frozen over.

"Think it's okay?" his friend Mitchell asked. Mitchell was a girl.

Garrett shrugged, then suddenly grinned. "My dad once said faith is like this." He waved at the ice as they both began to skate. "Like stepping out on ice without really knowing whether it will hold you."

They began to slap a puck back and forth to each other.

"Yeah. I thought you had to see God in order to believe in Him," Mitchell said after a while. "Now, I know you don't."

Neither spoke for a while, except to congratulate each other on a good shot. Finally Mitchell said, "Sometimes you can have faith in the wrong thing, though."

"Like what?"

"Like my dad said he had faith that I would be a boy, so he picked the name Mitchell. But I wasn't, and now I'm stuck with it!" Mitchell slapped the puck toward Garrett.

Your Turn

1. How would you describe faith in your own words?
2. In whom or what do you have faith?

Prayer

Jesus, I want to trust You as my Savior and have faith in You. I believe that You died to pay the price for my sins. Amen.

THE KEYS OF FAITH

If you've ever tried to learn to play the piano, you know that learning where the keys are is an important step. There are certain keys to faith as well. They can all be found in the Bible. These keys are lettered like the musical alphabet. Which of these keys do you know? How would you share this message with a friend?

A. For all have sinned and fall short of the glory of God (Romans 3:23).

B. For the wages of sin is death, but the gift of God is eternal life in Christ Jesus our Lord (Romans 6:23).

C. For God so loved the world that he gave his one and only Son, that whoever believes in him shall not perish but have eternal life (John 3:16).

D. But God demonstrates his own love for us in this: While we were still sinners, Christ died for us (Romans 5:8).

E. Faith is being sure of what we hope for and certain of what we do not see (Hebrews 11:1).

F. Without faith it is impossible to please God, because anyone who comes to him must believe that he exists and that he rewards those who earnestly seek him (Hebrews 11:6).

G. But the Counselor, the Holy Spirit, whom the Father will send in my name, will teach you all things and will remind you of everything I have said to you. And surely I am with you always, to the very end of the age (John 14:26; Matthew 28:20).

FAITH

God wants me to have faith when I pray.
*I tell you the truth, if you have faith as small as a mustard seed,
you can say to this mountain, "Move from here to there" and it
will move. Nothing will be impossible for you.*

Matthew 17:20

A Prayer of Faith

Arnie felt foolish. He wasn't even sure half the time that God existed, let alone listened when he prayed. Now it was his turn to lead the closing prayer in his Sunday school class. The teacher had a rule, though: no one had to pray aloud if he or she did not want to. You could say, "Pass," and the teacher would pray.

Arnie started to say, "Pass." In the split second that it would have taken him to say that word, the word "faith" came to mind. That was what they had discussed in class: faith in God, like having faith that God would hear you, even though you don't have any proof that He did. *I'm supposed to believe when I pray!* he thought.

"Arnie?" the teacher asked.

"Uh, I'm ready…God, help us believe that You hear us when we pray. Amen."

Before Arnie could escape after class, the teacher called him back. "Arnie, I know that's something you've been struggling with," she said.

Arnie nodded. "Yeah, but it kinda makes sense now. I can choose to believe that God hears me."

His teacher smiled. "Maybe you should teach the adult Sunday school class."

Your Turn

1. Why do you think God wants you to believe that He hears your prayers?
2. Do you believe He does? (Be honest!)

_____

_____

_____

Prayer

Lord, help me overcome my unbelief and have faith in You. Amen.

TELL ALL ABOUT IT

There comes a time in your life when you "own" your faith. That means you decide for yourself what you believe about God. Do you believe that God hears you when you pray? Complete the phrase below to explain what you believe.

I believe that God...

MY RELATIONSHIPS

FAMILY

Responsibility comes with the privilege of living with my family.
*Whatever you do, work at it with all your heart,
as working for the Lord, not for men.*

Colossians 3:23

Smells and Howls

Sam and Jordan were surprised to see their dad sitting on the back steps when they biked up the driveway. Their dog, Skipper, was sitting next to him and the cat was curled up in the sun. All that was missing was their mom. She was out of town on business for a few days.

"Hi, Dad, Skipper and Cleo," said Sam, nodding to each one. "Nice of you to greet us this way."

Skipper wagged his tail, Cleo ignored them and Mr. Adams stood up. When Jordan came up to the steps their dad said, "This isn't exactly a welcoming party. When I walked in the back door this afternoon I was met with bad smells and loud howls because the garbage can was overflowing and the pet dishes were empty."

"Oops!" said Sam. "I was late getting ready for school and had to rush. I guess I forgot to feed Cleo and Skipper. Sorry, fellas."

"I hate taking out the garbage," said Jordan. "So I decided to wait until the can was really, really full and then do it. Save some trips that way."

Mr. Adams told the boys to wait right there. Soon he returned with an alarm clock that wasn't running. He asked Sam to set the time. But the second hand didn't move, not even when the clock was shaken. When Jordan opened the back, they discovered the battery was missing.

"This clock is like our family," their father explained. "When some family members don't do their part, it affects the rest of the family. Everyone needs to work together to make good family relationships." Then Mr. Adams produced the missing battery. The clock started ticking.

Your Turn

1. How could the boys' neglect affect the family?
2. What responsibilities do you have in your family?
3. How is the rest of family affected if you don't do your job?

Prayer

Heavenly Father, thank You for putting me in a family. Help me to do my part in building good family relationships. Amen.

JOB JAR

What family chore do you dislike the most? Probably everyone in your family, including your mom and dad, has jobs they really hate doing. Try making the Job Jar and trading responsibilities for a week.

What You Need

- large glass jar with a lid
- slips of paper
- index card
- markers
- pencils
- stickers
- clear tape

What To Do

1. Clean a large glass jar and lid.

2. Write Job Jar on the index card in big letters. You can use the markers to decorate the label. Tape the label to the jar. The rest of the jar and the lid can be decorated with stickers.

3. Give each family member two or three slips of paper and ask them to write "hated" jobs on each slip. Fold the papers in half and put them in the Job Jar.

4. Once a week, have each family member pick a job from the jar. If you get your own, put it back and pick a different one. Do the job you picked for one week. You may find you like doing a job someone else hates!

FAMILY

God wants me to be a peacemaker in my family.
How good and pleasant it is when brothers live together in unity!
Psalm 133:1

Out of Tune

The Benson home was seldom quiet. Four kids, two cats, one dog and a bird raised the noise level to a dull roar. The talking, laughing, music and ringing phones were all a familiar, pleasant part of their daily family life. But sometimes not-so-pleasant sounds were heard in the Benson home.

Jack poked Jeff. Jeff poked back — harder. Soon they were wrestling on the floor, feet and arms flying in every direction. It didn't take long until they were yelling at each other: "Stop it!"

Greg teased Linda. Then Linda yelled, "Mom, Greg's bugging me! Tell him to leave me alone!" To emphasize her point, Linda went into her room and slammed the door.

Greg thought he should have the same privileges as Jack, even though he was two years older. The boys thought Linda got everything her way because she was a girl.

The one thing the whole Benson family loved doing together, though, was playing music. Their mom played piano, Dad played the clarinet and each of the kids played some kind of instrument.

One night Dad said, "Let's have a family concert." He handed out the music. It was a familiar song. Everyone tooted and plunked along harmoniously. Then they turned the page...what a horrible racket! Not only were they out of tune, there was no tune. The dog ran from the room.

"Not much harmony in that music," said Mr. Benson. "Everyone seemed to be doing their own thing instead of working together." Then he handed each of them the same second page instead of the six different songs he had given them before.

The kids got the point of Dad's musical demonstration as they played together in harmony.

Your Turn

1. What was causing disharmony in the Benson family?
2. How does your family resolve arguing?

_____

_____

Prayer

God of peace, help me to live in harmony with my family. Amen.

FAMILY HARMONY

Fill in the squares below, using the first letter of each object above the square. When you are finished, you will have written some of the things needed for family harmony. The answers are on page 247.

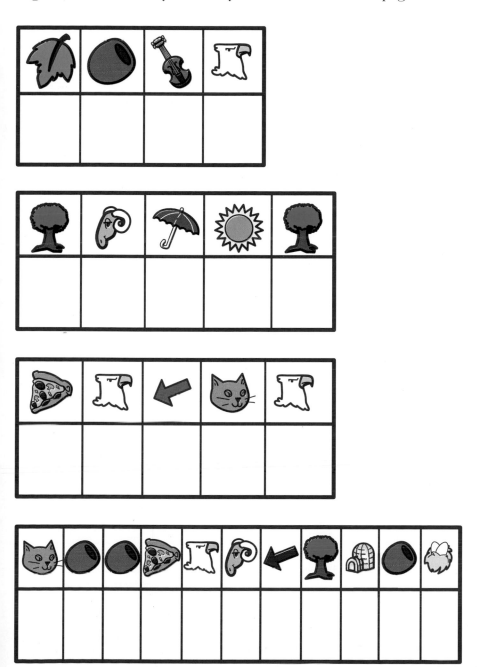

FRIENDS

Good friends help one another.
*Two are better than one... If one falls
down, his friend can help him up.*

Ecclesiastes 4:9-10

Ski Trip

Troy hesitated. He knew he should ask Kenny to come on the family ski trip. His aunt said he could ask a friend. And Kenny was his best friend. But Kenny was a terrible skier. He always asked a lot of questions. He also fell a lot.

Troy, on the other hand, was a great skier. He loved to ski! He just didn't like having to coach Kenny all the time. This is gonna be a drag with Kenny, he thought, as he stared at the phone. He dread calling Kenny.

"I sure wish my friend, Carol, could be with us on this trip," his aunt suddenly said. He hadn't realized she'd come into the room. "I sure miss being with her." She sighed.

Troy remembered how sad his aunt had been when her friend died. He suddenly felt bad that he hadn't wanted Kenny to come. He picked up the phone and dialed Kenny's number. He was soon so busy talking that he didn't see his aunt smile.

Your Turn

1. Who encouraged Troy to ask his friend to go on the trip? How?
2. How do you help your friends?
3. How do your friends help you?

_____

_____

_____

_____

_____

_____

Prayer

Lord, show me how to help my friends. Amen.

PRAYER FOR A FRIEND

One of the best ways to help a friend is to pray for him or her. Maybe there's a need that you can't meet for a friend, but there is nothing that God can't do. Keep a list of whom and what you pray for. Don't forget to list the answers.

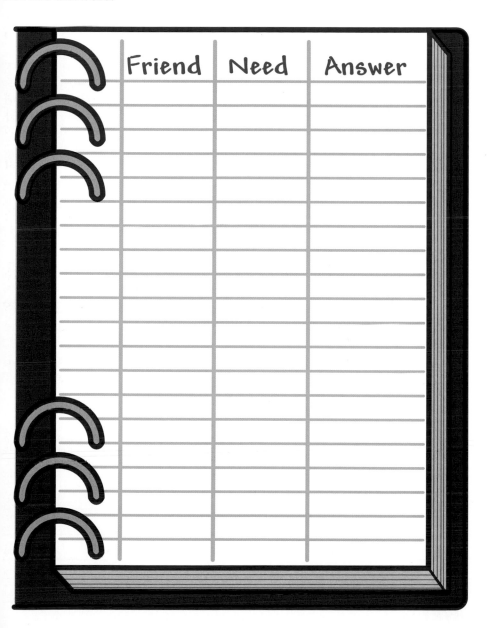

Friend	Need	Answer

FRIENDS

If I am a true friend, I will never abandon my friends.
Never abandon a friend — either yours or your father's.

Proverbs 27:10a, NLT

Jake's Choice

Jake couldn't believe it. Austin had called to invite him to a pool party at his house! Everybody in the sixth grade wanted to go to Austin's house. Practically the whole sixth grade was invited — except for Jake's friend Max. To Austin (and some of the other sixth graders), Max was a major geek.

Just as Jake celebrated the good news, Max called. "My dad's taking me to the movies on Saturday," Max said. "Want to come?"

Jake felt terrible. "Uh…I've been invited to Austin's."

Max groaned. "You too? Guess that means you don't wanna be my friend anymore."

"That's not true!"

"Yeah, sure." Max hung up soon after that.

Jake decided to pray and ask God what he should do. He didn't want to lose Max as a friend.

When Saturday came, Jake went to the party, but only stayed for half an hour. It turned out to be boring. He decided to go with Max to the movies after all.

"I'm sorry I got mad at you," Max said when Jake arrived. "I should've known that you still wanted to be my friend."

Your Turn

1. If you were Jake, would you have gone to the party? Why or why not?
2. Why is it important to "never abandon" a friend?
3. How can you be a friend who never abandons another?

_____

_____

_____

_____

Prayer

Lord, I want to stick with my friends. I can with Your help. Amen.

A MESSAGE FROM A FRIEND

The puzzle below is a message from a friend. Your friend's words are in John 15:14. Put the letters below each column in the boxes above that column. The letters may not be listed in the exact order in which they appear in the quote. Mark off used letters at the bottom. A letter may only be used once. Words may continue from one line to the next. The black boxes separate words. The answers are on page 247.

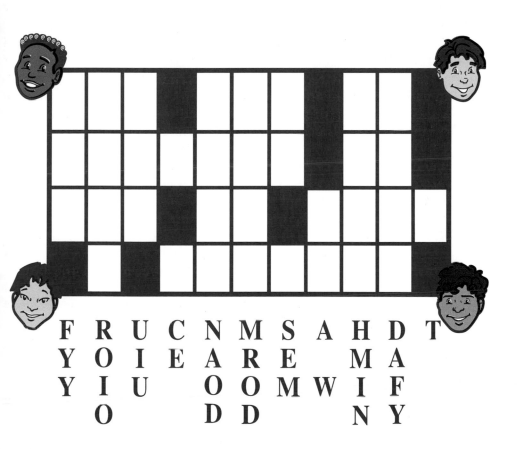

```
F   R   U   C   N   M   S   A   H   D   T
Y   O   I   E   A   R   E       M   A
Y   I   U       O   O   M   W   I   F
    O       D   D           N   Y
```

MY PLACE IN GOD'S FAMILY

As a Christian, I am an important person in God's family.
From [Christ] the whole body joined and held together by every
supporting ligament grows and builds itself up in love, as each
part does its work.

Ephesians 4:16

One Happy Family

We're all one big happy family, Sherman thought sarcastically. He didn't feel like he belonged to the body of Christ — at least not at this church. His family had recently started attending this new church. Sherman hadn't made any friends yet.

Now the fifth and sixth grade class wanted to do something for the church's anniversary. "Let's do a skit or something," someone had suggested.

Why should I even care what happens? Sherman thought. But as ideas were discussed, Sherman suddenly had a great idea for a skit. He wouldn't have said anything, but someone suddenly asked him if he had any ideas. In a small voice, Sherman told his idea.

"Hey, cool!" someone said. Other kids began to speak up excitedly.

"I can help you work on your skit," one boy said.

My skit? Sherman thought, suddenly remembering that the boy's name was Jason.

Others volunteered too. Before Sherman knew it, class time was over. For the first time since he'd started going to that church, he felt like he belonged.

Your Turn

1. In God's family, everyone has a place. What can you do to help other "family" members?
2. What has someone in God's family done to help you feel that you belong?

_____

_____

_____

Prayer

Jesus, I want to be a caring member of Your family. Amen.

YOUR FAMILY RIGHTS

What makes you think you belong to the family of God? John 1:12 does. To figure out the message, read the grid coordinates. Fill in the letters on the blanks. The first number is always the bottom number. The answer is on page 247.

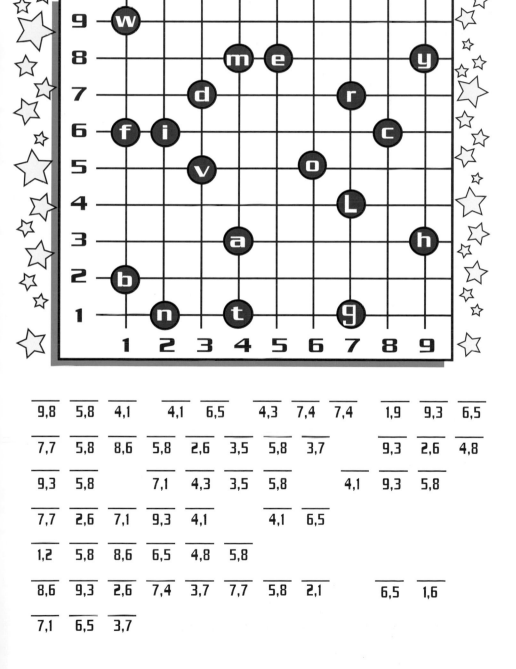

9,8	5,8	4,1		4,1	6,5		4,3	7,4	7,4	1,9	9,3	6,5

7,7 5,8 8,6 5,8 2,6 3,5 5,8 3,7   9,3 2,6 4,8

9,3 5,8   7,1 4,3 3,5 5,8   4,1 9,3 5,8

7,7 2,6 7,1 9,3 4,1   4,1 6,5

1,2 5,8 8,6 6,5 4,8 5,8

8,6 9,3 2,6 7,4 3,7 7,7 5,8 2,1   6,5 1,6

7,1 6,5 3,7

MY PLACE IN GOD'S FAMILY

Everyone is special in God's family.
*The body is a unit, though it is made up of many parts; and
though all its parts are many, they form one body.*

1 Corinthians 12:12

What's Special About Andrew?

Andrew Cornell listened to his brother singing in his room. Even though he'd just told his brother that he sounded like a walrus, Andrew knew that wasn't true. His brother had a great voice. He was often asked to sing at church. *Nobody asks me to sing*, Andrew thought. He knew his was a voice made for singing in the shower. *Nothing special about me.*

"Andy!" his father called from the kitchen. "I need your help, buddy."

"Okay, Dad!" Andrew went to see what his father wanted.

"Set the table, please. Dinner's almost ready."

"Okay." While Andrew got forks and knives, he asked, "What am I good at, Dad? Everybody around here gets asked to do stuff at church, but nobody ever asks me to do anything. Guess everybody thinks I'm just Billy's brother."

"That's not true. Not the part about your being Billy's brother. Just the other Sunday your teacher told me how much she enjoys having you in her class."

"Really?"

Mr. Cornell nodded. "You bet. Know why?"

Andrew shrugged.

"Because you're so helpful to the other kids. I always knew that about you. But that's not what makes you special. Know what does?"

"The fact that God made you Andrew Cornell."

Your Turn

1. What was special about Andrew?
2. What's special about you? (Think of at least two things.)

_____

_____

_____

Prayer

God, thanks for reminding me that I am special. Amen.

WHAT'S SPECIAL ABOUT THE FAMILY OF GOD?

To find out, shade in the areas that answer this question: Two sets of brothers were Jesus' disciples. Who were these four men? The answer is on page 247.

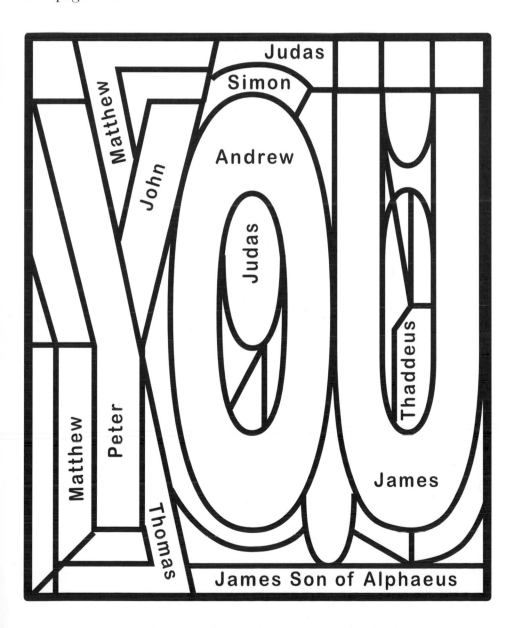

LOVING THE UNLOVELY

God loves every person and so should I.
For you are all one in Christ Jesus.

Galatians 3:28

Prickly Mr. Porcupine

All the boys watched as Jed hit the baseball over the fence into Mr. Zane's overgrown back yard.

"Guess the game is over because we have no more balls," said Jim. "Unless someone wants to go and ask Old Zany to give back our balls."

"No way!" said Jed. "I heard he yells at kids that come to the door."

"Maybe we should call him Prickly Mr. Porcupine because he's so grouchy and mean that no one wants to come near him," Jim hooted.

"Matt, you get the ball," said Jim. "Hope you survive."

Matt was nervous as he rang Mr. Zane's doorbell. The door opened a crack and an old man leaning on a cane looked out. "We hit a ball into your backyard. May I please look for it?" stuttered Matt.

Mr. Zane nodded his head and waved a gnarled hand at the back yard. Matt found the ball and two others they had lost. As he came back around the house, Mr. Zane was sitting on the front porch. He said, "You kids are pretty good ball players. I watch you from my porch. But you always leave before I can get to the ball and toss it back over the fence.

"I don't move very fast these days. But I used to be called Speedy Sam when I played minor league baseball. Boy could I run those bases! Now tell me about yourself," Mr. Zane said as he invited Matt to "sit a spell."

Soon Matt forgot all about Prickly Mr. Porcupine. He was having a great time listening to Mr. Zane's stories. He wasn't mean at all! When it was time to go, Matt said, "Why don't you come over and watch us tomorrow?"

"I'd be honored," Mr. Zane smiled. "I'll bring my old mitt and pick up any that roll my way."

Matt chuckled as he scooped up the three found balls and headed home.

Your Turn

1. How do you feel about old or sick people?
2. How does God want you to feel about them?

Prayer

God, thank You for loving everyone equally. Help me to do the same. Amen.

UNLOVELY PEOPLE

Jesus often associated with people that no one else wanted to be around. Jesus truly loved the unlovely — and He still does. To find out who some of these people were, cross out every G, H, J, Q, U, V, W, Y, Z in this puzzle. Write the words on the lines. The answer is on page 247.

G Z S I U V N Y Y N E J R Q S
T Z W A J U X V Z M H E Y G N
W D Z V E H G A F L U A M Z E
G H L J Q U E V P E Y Z R S H
Z U B H W L Z Z J I Q J N D V
Q P O Y Z O U R S W I J C Z K
G G I H N J Q S U A V N E W Z

_____

_____

_____

_____

_____

_____

LOVING THE UNLOVELY

I can show Jesus to others by loving them like He does.
Whatever you did for one of the least of these…you did for me.
Matthew 25:40

Choosing Sides

When Andrew entered the classroom, he noticed the new boy from Poland, Boris, sitting in the back. As usual, he was totally ignored. Class hadn't started yet so the fifth graders were talking and laughing. Everyone seemed to talk super fast, using lots of slang expressions and words. *This must be totally confusing to someone learning English like Boris,* Andrew thought.

Andrew walked to Boris's desk. He said, "Hi, I'm Andrew. I sure had trouble with today's math assignment. What did you think?"

After getting over the shock of someone talking to him, Boris said, "I like math. In my Polish school we had even harder work. I can help you." At lunchtime, Andrew saw Boris sitting alone and headed toward him.

"Hey, Drew, where are you going? We saved you a seat," called Doug.

"Why are you sitting with him? He can't talk to you," Carl said.

Andrew stopped by the crowded table. "I'm eating with Boris today. And he can speak English very well for just learning it. We probably wouldn't sound so great either if we had to speak Polish all of a sudden! And, Boris is a genius when it comes to math," he said.

After lunch, Ms. Conroy, the lunchroom monitor, came up to Andrew. "It was great how you stuck up for Boris. He needed help. And you gave the other kids something to think about," she said.

Your Turn

1. Do you know a "Boris"? How can you help him?
2. In the Scripture above, who are "the least of these?"

_____

_____

_____

_____

Prayer

God, help me to care for people others may not like. Amen.

THE LEAST OF THESE

Unscramble this Bible verse by carefully following these directions. The answer is on page 247.

1. Change K to a letter that sounds like part of the face.
2. Change O to H; V to K; Z to A; Q to P; D to M.
3. Change P to a letter that sounds like a personal pronoun.
4. Change W to a letter that sounds like the opposite of out.
5. Change J to R; Y to D; R to G; T to F; A to V.
6. Change M to a letter that sounds like a drink from China.
7. Change F to a well-rounded letter.
8. Change H to a letter that sounds like the Spanish word for yes.
9. Change B to the twelfth letter of the alphabet.
10. Change X to the sound a snake makes.
11. Change C to a letter that asks a question.
12. If you have followed the directions carefully, seven L's should remain. Change them to E.

I was _____ and you _____ me.
OPWRJC   TLY

I was _____ and you gave me a _____ .
MOKJXMC   YJKWV

I was a _____ and you _____ me
XMJZWRLJ   KWAKMLY

into your _____ . I was _____ and
OFDL   WZVLY

you gave me _____ . I was _____ and
HBFMOKWR   XKHV

you _____ for me. I was in _____ and
HZJLY   QJKXFW

you _____ me. (Matthew 25:35-36 NLT)
AKXKMLY

MY PLACE IN THE WORLD

God looks out for me, even when it seems that no one else does. *God has said, "Never will I leave you; never will I forsake you."*
Hebrews 13:5

The Sign

Mark and his friends Taro and Leslie headed to the convenience store in their neighborhood.

Leslie pointed to a sign on the door. " 'Only two kids allowed in the store at a time,' " she read. "That's not fair."

"If you kids wouldn't steal, then they wouldn't have to put up a sign," a woman said as she went into the store.

Mark, Taro and Leslie all exclaimed indignantly, "We don't steal!!"

The woman acted as if she didn't care.

"I wanted to get some potato chips," Leslie said. "But I don't want to shop here."

"We could walk down to the grocery store," Taro suggested.

"That's two miles away! I knew we should've brought our bikes!" Mark said.

Suddenly a familiar red van pulled up. Taro's father leaned out the window. "I was headed home when I saw you three. Want a ride?" he asked.

Taro was glad to see his father. "We were gonna walk down to the grocery store. At least they still allow all three of us there." He pointed to the sign.

"Well, at least you know that God is still looking out for you," said his father.

Your Turn

1. How did God provide for Mark and his friends?
2. How would you describe your world?
3. What are some ways that God shows His care of you?

Prayer

Lord, thanks for watching out for me. Amen.

WHAT DO YOU THINK?

God cares about your concerns and your world. Read each sentence starter. Write your thoughts in each space. Then pray about them.

If you could change...

your neighborhood, what would it be like? Why?

_____

_____

your school, what would it be like? Why?

_____

_____

the world, what would you be like? Why?

_____

_____

yourself, what would you be like? Why?

_____

_____

MY PLACE IN THE WORLD

God knows all the circumstances of my life.
*For he is our God and we are the people of his
pasture, the flock under his care.*

Psalm 95:7

Change Is Good

"Turned you down, huh?" Zane asked.

Marvin slammed his petition on the desk in the family room and glared at his older brother. "I don't see anything wrong with being able to stay up an hour later. You get to stay up," he huffed.

Zane laughed. "That's 'cause I'm almost 16. You're only 11, squirt."

Older brothers are a pain, Marvin thought. "I wish I were older sometimes."

"You'll get there. I gotta hand it to you. I never would've thought of the petition thing."

Marvin looked pleased. "I got the idea out of a book. I got all of my friends to sign it. We're all trying to get our parents to let us stay up longer." His face fell. "At least it worked in the book. It's not fair!"

Zane laughed. "Cheer up. There are worse things that could happen." He threw a pillow at Marvin, which hit him on the shoulder. "See? You could get hit by a pillow."

"You're in for it!"

Your Turn

1. What change did Marvin want to make?
2. Do you ever feel that life isn't fair? When are the times that you're most tempted to feel that way?

_____

_____

_____

_____

Prayer

God, sometimes the circumstances of my world aren't fair. Thanks for making a difference, though, in my life. Amen.

A PROMISE FROM THE SHEPHERD

Read the passage below. Really think about what it says. This is a promise you can count on, no matter what changes in your world.

[1] The Lord is my shepherd, I shall not be in want. [2] He makes me lie down in green pastures, he leads me beside quiet waters, [3] he restores my soul. He guides me in paths of righteousness for his name's sake. [4] Even though I walk through the valley of the shadow of death, I will fear no evil, for you are with me; your rod and your staff, they comfort me. [5] You prepare a table before me in the presence of my enemies. You anoint my head with oil; my cup overflows. [6] Surely goodness and love will follow me all the days of my life, and I will dwell in the house of the Lord forever.

~ Psalm 23

MY JOURNEY WITH GOD

PRAYER

Praying is having a personal talk with God.
The prayer of a righteous man is powerful and effective.

James 5:16

Heart to Heart Talk

Each kid in the sixth grade Bible study was given a word to explain to the others at the next class. Kevin's word was "prayer." *I already know how to pray,* he thought. He was still thinking about it when Uncle Jack called. "Can you help me build this deck for a while?" he asked.

Kevin and Uncle Jack made so much noise sawing and hammering they could hardly hear each other talk. When they finally took a break, Uncle Jack asked, "Hey, Kev, what's new with you?"

Kevin said, "Not much. You know, same old thing — school, home, friends. Wait. There's something new in Bible study but my part is pretty much the same old thing there too." Kevin explained the project to his uncle.

"I've been praying forever," said Kevin. "What more can I learn?"

Uncle Jack told Kevin to look around the half-finished deck. Then he asked, "What's the most important part?"

"Plans and measuring things exactly," Kevin decided.

"That's important," his uncle agreed. "But the most important part of this deck is the nails. Without them nothing would stay in place. Prayer is sort of like nails. It holds your Christian life together. Prayer is like having a heart to heart talk with God. You can talk to Him about anything and everything, good or bad. "

As they went back to work Kevin said, "Think I'll do double duty. As I bang these nails, I'll think of someone or something that I can pray about. These may be some of the noisiest prayers ever!"

Your Turn

1. How do you feel about prayer? When do you pray?
2. Why is praying important in a Christian's life?

Prayer

God, I'm glad I can always talk to You anytime, anywhere and for anything. Thanks for always listening. Amen.

PRAYER POWER

Fit one letter in each column into a square above the column. A colored square means the end of a word. When you have solved the puzzle, read across the squares to discover what God says about prayer. The answers are on page 247.

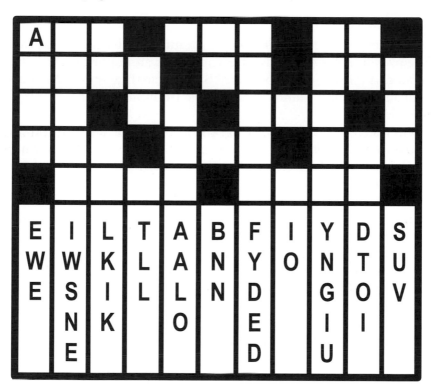

When do you pray?

_____

Where do you pray?

_____

What do you pray for?

_____

PRAYER

I can ask God to help others.
Call upon me in the day of trouble; I will deliver you.

Psalm 50:15

News Flash!

Brian was sprawled on the floor watching the basketball playoffs on TV. The program was suddenly interrupted for an important news flash. A serious-faced announcer reported, "Strong earthquakes have shaken a string of small Pacific islands. Thousands are homeless and hundreds are feared dead."

While the reporter was talking, pictures of the destruction flashed onto the screen. People were walking around in a daze amid the rubble of their homes. Small children were crying for their parents and hurt people were lying on the sides of the roads waiting for help.

"Man, I really don't like this," Brian said to his dad.

"This is a major news story," Mr. Clark explained. "The basketball game will be back on soon."

Brian interrupted, "I don't care about the game right now. Seeing that news flash made me feel scared and sad. I hate hearing and seeing about terrible things. Maybe if I never watched TV it would be better."

"Well, I don't think you'll do that," his father answered. "Not watching tragedies and bad news on TV won't improve anything. As long as there's sin in the world, all kinds of terrible things will keep right on happening. But there's one thing we can do about it."

"What's that?" Brian asked.

Mr. Clark continued, "We can pray for people in trouble. God promises to hear our prayers and help those in need. Let's pray for the earthquake victims right now."

Brian and his father bowed their heads to ask God to help the earthquake victims.

Your Turn

1. How do you feel when you hear or read distressing news stories?
2. How can you help people you don't know?

_____

_____

Prayer

Merciful Father, please help people that have trouble. Amen.

PRAYING FOR OTHERS

God promises to hear our prayers and to help those who are in need. If you read about someone in the newspaper or hear about someone on TV who needs God's help, pray for him or her. You can pray for anyone, even people you don't know. God knows everyone in the whole world. He wants us to pray for each other and for anyone who has trouble. Fill in the blanks of the prayer below. Use it as you pray for others, or make up your own prayer.

Dear God,

Sometimes I feel sad or scared or angry when I hear or read about all the terrible things that happen in the world.

Today I want to pray for

_____

_____

because this has happened to them:

_____

_____

Please help them and be with them. Thank You, God, for Your love for all people. In Jesus' name. Amen.

READING GOD'S WORD

God talks to me through His Word.
Direct my footsteps according to your word;
let no sin rule over me.

Psalm 119:133

When God Speaks

Dale had his Bible open, but didn't hear a word. Not one sound from God. "I thought God spoke through His Word," he complained to his father. He had just entered the family room where Dale lay sprawled on the couch.

"He does," he said.

"I've been reading this for 10 whole minutes. I haven't heard God say one word."

Her father chuckled. "He does help you understand what He wants you to do. Sometimes it helps to be quiet and listen. What are you reading?"

"The story of the lost son. I'm at the part where the mean older brother didn't want his brother to have a party."

"Kinda like the time when you didn't want us to take your brother out to celebrate his finally getting a C on his report card instead of his usual D in math."

"But that wasn't fair, Dad. I get A's all the time and you only took me out once."

"I think God is speaking to you through this story, Dale. Maybe you're not really listening."

Your Turn

1. What do you think God was telling Dale?
2. How has God directed your footsteps through His Word, as the memory verse mentions?
3. What will you do this week to find out more through God's Word?

_____

_____

_____

Prayer

Lord, thank You for Your Word. Amen.

A SAFE PLACE TO HIDE

What's the best place for God's Word? Psalm 119:11 gives you the low down. The answers are on page 247.

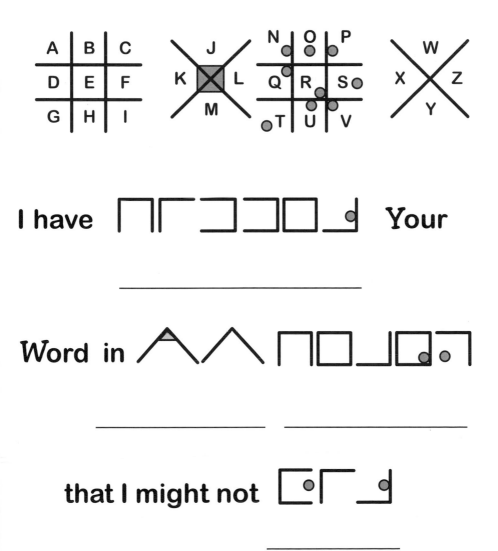

I have ⌐⌐⌐ ⊐⊐☐⌐ Your

_____

Word in ∧∧∧ ⌐☐⊐☐⌐

_____   _____

that I might not ⌐○⌐⌐

_____

against You.

READING GOD'S WORD

God directs my path through His Word.
Your word is a lamp to my feet and a light for my path.
Psalm 119:105

Written Road Map

"Habakkuk!" Carey slammed his Bible shut. "It figures Joanie knew where it is. I can barely pronounce that book let alone spell it."

"I never heard of it," his friend George said. "You're sure it's in the Bible?"

"Having trouble?" their small group leader asked.

"Why do we have these Scripture drills? Joanie wins all the time." He made a face at Joanie, who sat at the next table, smirking.

"That's because she knows the books of the Bible. The Scripture drills are just a fun way to get you exposed to the books."

"Yeah, but who's gonna read Habakkuk? Nobody can find it!"

Some of the kids laughed.

"The whole Bible is like a road map, Carey. Every book contains a part of God's plan. This is how He directs our steps each day. Habakkuk's like a little side street on a map. You may not think it's important, but someday, you might need to go there."

Your Turn

1. Why is the Bible like a road map?
2. How has the Bible helped you recently?

_____

_____

_____

_____

_____

_____

Prayer

Lord, when I'm tempted to doubt, help me to believe that I can get good advice from Your Word. Amen.

WHAT'S GREAT ABOUT THE WORD?

Glad you asked. Solve the rebus and find out. (2 Timothy 3:16a).
Check out the rest of 2 Timothy 3:16. How does knowing this change
the way you respond to the Bible? The answers are on page 247.

(2Timothy 3:16a)

OBEYING GOD

Obedience to God is a command, not a request.
Keeping God's commands is what counts.

1 Corinthians 7:19b

Way to Obey

"Are you listening to me?"

Claude never liked it when his mother said that. "Yeah," he said. He glanced at her as she stood in the doorway to his room.

"Good," she said. "I suggest you have all of your chores done by the time I get back from the store or else."

Claude nodded. He knew that tone. His mother wasn't really suggesting that he do it. She expected him to do it. He knew what "or else" meant: he would be grounded for one thing. No TV or video games for another. He also knew she only said "or else" the second time she had to tell him to do something.

His glance fell on the devotional his mother had bought for him. Today's topic was "Why obey God?"

Everybody wants me to obey, he thought, followed by a sigh out loud. Why can't I order someone around?

Another word caught his eye: love.

He knew his mother loved him, even though she expected him to do things like chores. *Maybe God is like that too,* he thought.

Your Turn

1. What do you think obedience to God means?
2. What do you find hard and/or easy about obeying God?

_____

_____

_____

_____

_____

_____

Prayer

Lord, help me to obey Your commands. Amen.

HIS WAY TO OBEY

If Bible people would have kept reminder notes on their refrigerators (they didn't because they didn't even have refrigerators then!), which of the following building projects would these notes represent? Write the building names next to the notes. Then write the names of those who would use each note to show how he obeyed God. The answer is on page 247.

1. The temple
2. The ark
3. The tabernacle

A. Noah
B. Solomon
C. Moses/Aaron

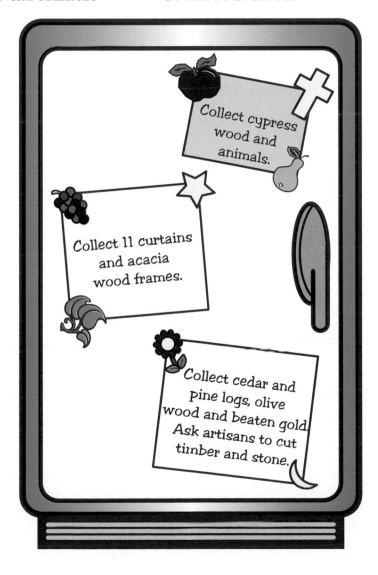

OBEYING GOD

Obeying God is something I should
do all the time, not just sometimes.
If you love me, you will obey what I command.

John 14:15

That's Telling Him!

"You go to church every Sunday?" Steve acted like he couldn't believe what Faith had just said.

Faith nodded, not wanting to talk to Steve. She had wandered into the family room where Steve was waiting on her brother.

"No wonder they call you 'Faith.' " Steve laughed at his own joke.

"Doofus" was on the tip of Faith's tongue, but she bit the name back in time. *My brother's friends are so dumb,* she thought before she said, "There's nothing wrong with going to church every Sunday. Lots of people do it."

"We only go twice a year — Christmas and Easter."

She rolled her eyes. "Don't you believe in God? You're supposed to do what He says all the time."

Steve finally went off with her brother. "Can you believe Clark's friends?" she asked her older sister Karen.

"Faith, you said something about doing what God says, but you sure don't act like you believe that," said Karen.

"What do you mean?"

"You were kind of snotty to Steve just now."

Faith sighed. "He is a total goofball!"

"Yes, but what about 'Judge not.' Isn't that one of Jesus' commands? Aren't you supposed to obey that all the time?"

"Why do I bother talking to you?" Faith hated to admit that her sister was right.

Your Turn

1. Is obedience to God something you would want to do? Why or why not?

_____

_____

2. What do you believe about obedience to God?(Circle a response below.)

**I do it all the time,
no questions asked.**

**Sometimes I find
obeying Him to be hard.**

Prayer

Lord, help me to trust You enough to obey. Amen.

WHY OBEY?

Obedience is sometimes difficult. As humans, we like to be in charge. But there's one reason why God wants us to obey Him. Use the Morse code below to figure out why. The answer is on page 247.

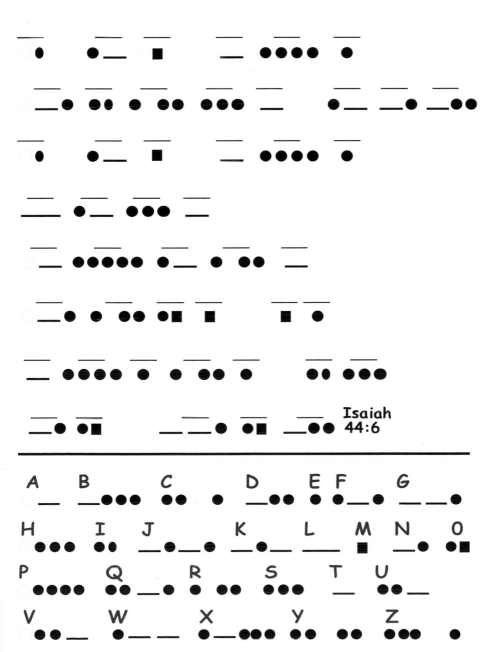

PRAISE AND WORSHIP

I should praise God to thank Him for what He does for me.
Great is the Lord and most worthy of praise.

Psalm 145:3

The Joy Factor

Ken usually liked Sundays. The whole family went to church and to Sunday school. Many times they stopped at a restaurant for lunch on the way home. Sunday afternoons were quiet — good for reading or just doing nothing.

But this wasn't a good Sunday. Ken had been embarrassed in the junior high Sunday school class when he tripped and almost fell. Then his voice squeaked when he sang in church. Ken was sure everyone heard him. To top off the morning, he spilled gravy on his pants in the restaurant.

Ken slouched in the living room chair, reading the Sunday comics and feeling sorry for himself. Then his little sister, Katie, marched into the room. She sang "Alleluia" over and over in her loudest 4-year-old voice.

"Enough already!" Ken said. "Nothing to 'Alleluia' about!"

Katie stomped her foot and went to find their mom. *Oh, great,* thought Ken. *Now I'll get chewed out, too.* When Mrs. Bartlett came into the room, she didn't say anything, just handed him a small mirror. When Ken looked at himself he saw a grumpy looking kid with a big frown on his face. "It takes more muscles to frown than to smile," his mother said. "I think your joy factor is about zero right now. Want to talk about it?"

Ken told his mom about his miserable morning and that he didn't feel like hearing Katie's "Alleluia." "I think you need to hear it and think about it," said Mrs. Bartlett. "Alleluia is sort like saying 'hooray' to God. God loves you all the time and does lots of wonderful things for you. He deserves thanks and praise for all His blessings. You can do that even when you feel like the clumsiest, sloppiest, most squeaky-voiced kid that ever lived."

Ken's smile muscles started working as he thought about the good parts of the day instead of the bad ones.

Your Turn

1. How do you praise God?
2. For what do you praise God?

Prayer

Alleluia, alleluia, alleluia. Praise ye the Lord. God, You are great! Amen.

ALLELUIA

"Alleluia" is sort of like saying "hooray" to God. Use each letter in the puzzle below to name some of the things God gives you for which you want to praise and thank Him. For example, next to the A you might write "All my family and friends."

A _____

L _____

L _____

E _____

L _____

U _____

I _____

A _____

PRAISE AND WORSHIP

I can worship God anytime.
Sing to the Lord, praise his name; proclaim
his salvation day after day.

Psalm 96:2

Everyday Worship

"This sure is one huge blooper," Zach muttered. "They definitely need some better editors for this book."

His mom looked up from the newspaper. "Were you talking to me?" she asked.

"No," Zach answered. "I was talking to myself. But maybe you can help me figure out something."

"I'll do my best," Mom said as she laid down the paper. "What's the problem?"

"I'm doing a page in this book for Bible Club," Zach explained. "The whole lesson is about worship and the different parts of the church service. But this question asks 'How do you worship God every day?' I think they meant to say 'on Sunday.' I don't go to church every day, so this question is impossible to answer." Zach gave a big sigh and closed the book.

"Zach, there's nothing wrong with the book," his mother explained. "You don't have to be in church to worship God. You worship Him every time you pray or sing songs of praise. It's even worshipping God when we obey Him and do what's pleasing to Him. We have church services so everyone can worship God together, but you can also worship Him all alone."

"Hmmm," Zach said. "I never thought of it that way — think I'll call it 'everyday worship.' "

Your Turn

1. How do you worship God in church?
2. How do you worship God when you're not in church?
3. Why does God deserve to be worshipped?

_____

_____

_____

Prayer

Dear God, help me to worship You in church and in my everyday life. Amen.

PSALM 100

Psalm 100 is a psalm for giving thanks. It is a psalm of worship and praise. Fit the green words into the puzzle. The answer is on page 247.

Shout for joy to the Lord, all the earth.
Worship the Lord with gladness;
Come before him with joyful songs.
Know that the Lord is God.
It is he who made us, and we are his;
we are his people, the sheep of his pasture.
Enter his gates with thanksgiving and his courts with praise;
give thanks to him and praise his name.
For the Lord is good and his love endures forever;
his faithfulness continues through all generations.

REPENTANCE

Real repentance means turning away from wrongdoing.
Create in me a clean heart, O God,
and renew a steadfast spirit within me.

Psalm 51:10

Do You Mean It?

"Do you really mean it when you say you're sorry?"

The junior high group leader's question stuck in Tom's mind. He'd just told his uncle he was sorry after being caught in a lie. He had lied about why he'd been late coming home from school. Being sent to the principal's office was not something he had wanted to tell his uncle.

"Tom, that's the second time you've lied to me this week," his uncle had reminded him. "You know that lying is wrong."

Tom had promised that he wouldn't lie again. Now he wondered if he would be able to keep that promise.

"If you know you have a problem, you can ask God to help you turn away from wrong," the youth leader said. "First, just admit you can't do it on your own."

During prayer time, Tom did just that. Afterwards, he felt better. He caught up with his uncle after church.

"Uh, I'm sorry I was late this week...and for lying and stuff." Tom couldn't look him in the eye.

"You already told me you were sorry."

"Yeah, but...this time...I really mean it."

Your Turn

1. What helped to change Tom's mind about the way he treated his uncle?
2. Repentance means turning away from wrongdoing. Have you ever done something you knew was wrong? How can you keep from doing the same thing over and over?

_____

_____

_____

Prayer

Jesus, I want to mean it when I say I'm sorry. Help me turn from all wrongdoing. Amen.

A FRESH START

Would you like a fresh start? Two words can start you on your way: "I'm sorry." This is one way to erase your mistakes and start over. Is there someone to whom you need to say those words? God, maybe? Use the space below to be on your way to a fresh start.

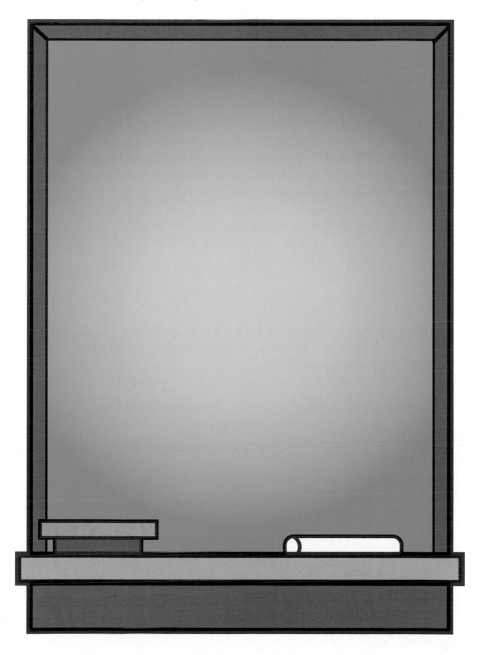

REPENTANCE

Everyone has sinned and needs to turn to God for salvation.
Turn to me and be saved, all you ends of the earth;
for I am God, and there is no other.

Isaiah 45:22

Bumper Sticker

"Hey, Dad, look at that bumper sticker." Kenneth Simmons pointed to the car ahead.

" 'I'm my own Savior,' " his father read with disgust. "Huh. I've seen more clever bumper stickers that were just as wrong." He shot Kenneth a glance. "What would you put on a bumper sticker?"

Kenneth shrugged. He couldn't drive, so he didn't much care. Now if he had his own car..." 'I like video games?' "

Mr. Simmons smiled. "I meant about God."

Kenneth shrugged again. "What would you put, Dad?" He knew his father would tell him anyway. He didn't actually mind.

" 'A person who needs a Savior can't be his own Savior.' "

"Aren't we all just basically good?"

"Where did you hear that?"

Kenneth shrugged a third time. "Somebody said that at school. Said she heard it on some show on TV."

"Kenneth, you know we've all sinned. It could be a lie or a harmful thought about someone. We were born in sin. Are you sure you're not wondering about this yourself?"

Kenneth looked at his father. Instead of shrugging, he gave a sheepish grin.

Your Turn

1. Why can't we save ourselves?
2. If you could put a message about repentance on a bumper sticker, what would you? Why?

_____

_____

_____

Prayer

God, thank You for the salvation You offer when we repent. Amen.

YOUR MESSAGE

Look back at question 2. Now is your chance to do what it says. Use the space below to write your message. Include pictures as well.

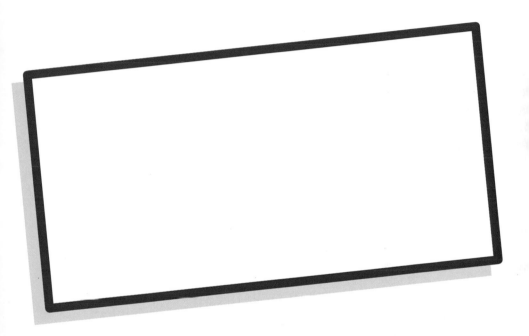

ABIDING IN CHRIST

Abiding in Christ starts with getting to know Him.
I keep asking that the God of our Lord Jesus Christ, the glorious Father, may give you the Spirit of wisdom and revelation, so that you may know him better.

Ephesians 1:17

Meet My Friend

"I wish I could meet him," Denny said, waving the sports magazine at his friend Tyler.

"Who?" Tyler barely glanced up from the video game in his hands. He already knew who. Denny only talked about one person — his favorite baseball player. "What would you do if you could?" he asked.

Denny shrugged. "Get to know him, I guess. Hang with him."

Tyler put the game on pause. "I've got someone you can meet. All you have to do is come to church with my family on Sunday."

Denny's eyes glazed over. "What? Not again."

"Really, this friend is way cool. All my friends at church think so, once they've gotten to know him."

"Does he play baseball?"

Tyler only laughed.

Denny grinned. "I already know the punch line. God, right?"

Tyler went back to the game. "Wanna come? Church is fun. God's cool, too, when you get to know Him. You've gotta stick with Him, though."

Your Turn

1. Who is the person you would most like to meet? Why?
2. Why is it important to stick with Jesus?
3. How have you gotten to know Jesus? If you don't know Him, use the prayer below. Even if you do know Him, use the prayer below.

_____

_____

_____

_____

Prayer

Dear God, I want to know Jesus as my Savior. Help me to stick with Him, even when others don't. Amen.

THE SECRET

Psst! Come closer. That's good. Want to know the secret to abiding in Christ? Hold the bottom of the page so that it is level with your nose. Then, turn the book so that the side of the page is level with your nose. You'll find a sure-fire way to stay with Jesus.

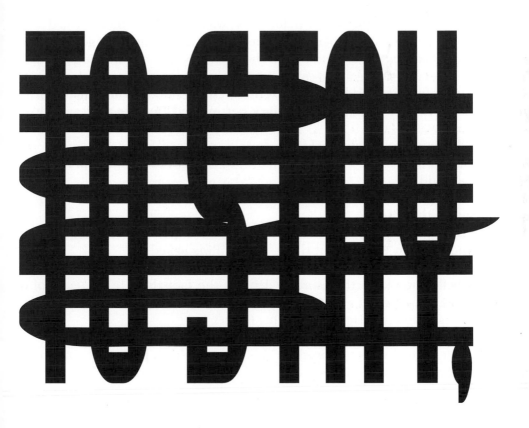

ABIDING IN CHRIST

Abiding in Christ means accepting that He is in control.
Remain in my love.

John 15:9b

The Answer

Jesse Collins silently followed the rest of the family to the van. He could hardly believe that Uncle Gary was dead. He had prayed and prayed, asking God to make him better. Now Uncle Gary was gone.

Jesse's father put a hand on his shoulder. "You're awful quiet, buddy."

"I'll never pray again," Jesse said.

Mr. Collins paused before answering, "Never's a long time. Why?"

"I asked God to make Uncle Gary better. And He didn't." Jesse wiped tears away.

"You guys go on ahead. I want to talk to Jesse," his father said to the others. He led Jesse to a stone bench. "Jesse, right now you're pretty mad at God, huh?"

Jesse nodded. God had let Uncle Gary die. His uncle was his favorite person in the world.

"Remember how you told me that Jesus was your Savior and that you wanted to know more about Him?" Mr. Collins asked.

Jesse reluctantly nodded.

"Well, one of the things about Him is the fact that He's in control of our lives. That's what we agree to when we ask Him into our lives. We also agree that whatever He does is right. Right?"

Jesse shrugged.

"You know I miss my brother," his father said as he wiped away tears of his own. "But I know, Jess, that God is still in control."

Your Turn

1. What answer did Jesse receive to his prayer: yes, no or maybe?
2. When are you most tempted to let go of God, instead of sticking with Him? Why?

_____

_____

_____

Prayer

Lord, help me to accept the fact that You're in control of my life. Amen.

FRUIT BASKET UPSET

When you stick with Jesus, you bear fruit. Does that mean you turn into a pear tree? No. But you do gain these. Unscramble the words to find out what you gain from Galatians 5:22-23. The answers are on page 247.

Ovle_____

Oyj_____

ecape_____

catenipe_____

dinksens _____

nodseogs_____

thaiffensuls_____

neteslengs_____

lefs-tooncrl_____

Fruit doesn't come up overnight! Which of these will you need to help you wait for God to work in your life?

_____

_____

_____

LIVING IN HARMONY

God wants me to get along with others.
Live in harmony with one another; be sympathetic, love as brothers, be compassionate and humble.

1 Peter 3:8

Handling Things Peacefully

"Keep your junk off my side of the room." Richard Kean threw a bowling shoe at his twin brother's bed.

"I said I was sorry!" Ray yelled.

"Can't we all just get along?!" their mother cried as she appeared in the doorway. "What's with you two?"

"He keeps tearing up my stuff!" Richard held up the hand-held video game. It was slightly cracked.

"You're fighting over something that cost $19.99?" Mrs. Kean shook her head. "Look, you guys, what did I tell you about handling things peacefully? It's important to try to get along. I don't want to hear you two fighting every two minutes like this."

"If he would just ask before taking my stuff," Richard said.

Mrs. Kean threw Ray a look. "Ray, I told you about that."

"I just looked at it for a second."

"Ray…"

"Okay! Okay!"

Mrs. Kean turned to Richard. "And Rich, stop getting so mad over little things, okay?"

Richard sighed. "Okay."

"Now kiss and make up." She paused, then laughed at the sight of their stricken faces. "Just kidding!"

Your Turn

1. What kept Ray and Richard from getting along?
2. Living in harmony means keeping the peace with everyone. What are some things you can do to live in harmony with your family?

_____

_____

_____

Prayer

Lord, help me live in harmony with others. Amen.

THINKING LIKE HIM

Living in harmony with others isn't always easy. It means you can't always have your way and they can't always have their way. It means making choices. God can help you. How? By helping you to think like Jesus. How? First Corinthians 2:16 has that promise. But, you have to figure that out by figuring out the rebus below. Some words are sound-alikes. The answers are on page 247.

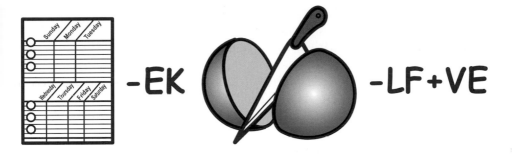

THE

LIVING IN HARMONY

God helps me live peacefully with others.
Live in peace with each other.

1 Thessalonians 5:13

Competition

"Okay! Time!" Jim, the youth leader, blew his whistle. "You guys..."
He looked at all of the junior highers in front of him, especially Brian.

Brian had come up with idea to team the boys against the girls. But
soon arguments had begun.

"The whole idea of Game Night is to have fun," Jim said. "None of you
look like you're having fun. Except for Brian."

"The girls are just mad because we're beating them four games to
two," Brian declared.

"You cheat!" a girl named Vanessa yelled.

"Yeah!" the other girls agreed.

Jim waved his hand for quiet. "The whole idea is to have fun. But
getting along with each other is a goal we need to keep in mind. That's
what God wants. Now what do you think He'd want you to do in this
situation?"

"He'd want Brian to stop cheating!" Vanessa yelled.

"He'd also want everyone to think about what he or she..." Jim looked
hard at Vanessa, "...could do to get along with others."

"Okay! I'll stop saying Brian's cheating," Vanessa suggested.

"Good idea. Any other suggestions?" Jim asked.

"I'll stop cheating!" Brian said. Everyone laughed.

Your Turn

1. What needs to happen for everyone to get along?
2. What can you do to live peacefully with others?

_____

_____

_____

_____

Prayer

Lord, help me do what it takes to get along with others at home, at school
— anywhere. Amen.

ANCIENT HIEROGLYPHICS?

The text on the wall below is not some newly discovered Egyptian hieroglyphics. Cross out the Xs, Ys and Ns to discover items you can give to encourage peaceful relations anywhere. The answers are on page 247.

EVANGELISM

I can share Jesus by being myself.
In [Christ] we live and move and have our
being....We are his offspring.

Acts 17:28

A Life Shared

"Hey, Raul! Where are you going?"

Raul Guiterrez dreaded the sound of that voice. Not today, he thought. Just as he was on his way to youth church, he had to run into Caesar Hujar! Caesar was one of the toughest kids in the apartment complex. Raul didn't want Caesar to call him names just because he was going to church.

"Didn't you hear me, man?" Caesar asked.

"Yeah." Raul sounded defensive. He didn't know what to say to Caesar. His mother had once suggested that he invite Caesar to church. *Yeah, right,* he had thought then.

A new thought came to his mind now. *Pray.*

What do I say, God? he prayed. Suddenly he knew. All he had to do was be himself. He didn't have to be ashamed of going to church.

"I'm going to Parkside," he finally said. Parkside was the church in the neighborhood.

"You go there?" Caesar looked surprised. "Wow...maybe I'll go there sometime."

Raul thought he would die of shock and relief. "How 'bout today?"

Your Turn

1. What is the hardest thing about telling others about Jesus?
2. Who is the last person you think you'd talk to about Jesus? Why?

_____

_____

_____

_____

_____

Prayer

Dear God, You made me who I am. Let my life show that I trust Jesus. Amen.

DO-IT-YOURSELF TRACT

Use the blank card below to share the gospel message with someone. First, photocopy this page or scan it into your computer and print it. Cut out the card around the solid lines and fold the two sides inward. Then fold the top and bottom inward. Then open the flaps and write your message underneath them. You could write a Bible verse or a special message about God. Pray about who would benefit from receiving the card. Then fold the card back together and secure the flaps with tape.

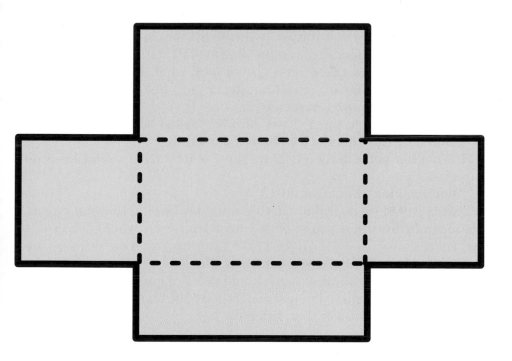

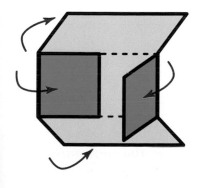

EVANGELISM

I can show others how important Jesus is to me.
Let your light shine before men, that they may see your good
deeds and praise your Father in heaven.

Matthew 5:16

The T-Shirt

"Mom, I can't wear this." Ethan Miniver held up the T-shirt his mother had just given him.

"What's wrong with a WWJD T-shirt?" his mother asked. "I think it's cute. It'll get your friends to wonder what WWJD stands for."

Ethan's eyes had taken on a glazed look when his mother said the word "cute." Now they blazed with indignation. "See, that's what I mean. They'll be asking me what it means."

"Why is that a bad thing?" Mrs. Miniver looked puzzled.

"They'll be thinking I'm a weirdo or something."

His mother paused, then held up the T-shirt. "What would Jesus do?" she asked.

"Mommmmm," Ethan whined.

"What would He do, Ethan, in this situation? Would He want you to be ashamed of Him when you're with your friends? Or would He...you tell me."

Ethan shrugged. "I'm not ashamed of Him."

"Then what do you think you should do? I'm not so concerned about your wearing this T-shirt. I'm just concerned about how important He is to you. Only you can answer that, Ethan."

Your Turn

1. How important do you think Jesus is to Ethan? How can you tell?
2. Is Jesus important to you? How do your actions show that this is true?

Prayer

Lord, I want my light to shine before people as the Scripture above suggests. Amen.

WWYD (WHAT WOULD YOU DO)?

What message would you put on a T-shirt to show what you believe about Jesus? Use the one below to write or draw your message. Is this something you would wear? Why or why not?

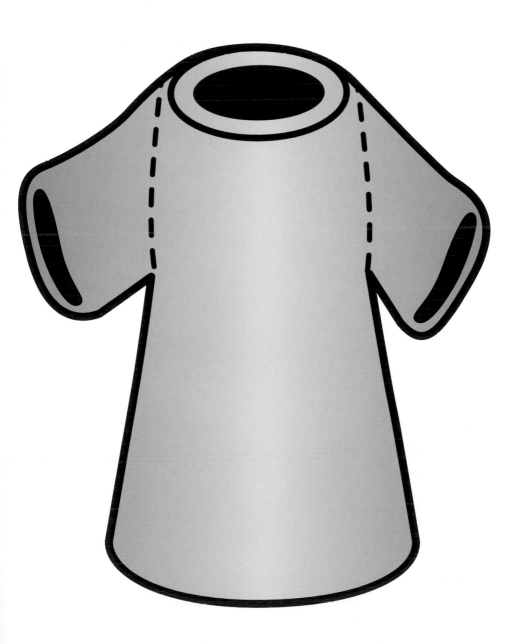

MY WORLD IS GOD'S WORLD

LEARNING ABOUT GOD'S CREATION

God wants me to care for His creation.
Rule over the fish...the birds...and over every living creature.
Genesis 1:28

All God's Creatures

"Most of the time, I'm glad I live on a farm," Cody said to his dad as they repaired a hole in the fence. "But these goats are a big pain. They're always getting out and running all over the place. Mom really gets mad when they chomp on her garden, too. Maybe we could sell them."

Mr. Daniels laughed as he gave the fence wire a final twist. "These goats are just being goats," he said. "They like to jump and run and have fun. But we make money selling their milk. I think we'll keep them."

Cody and his dad sat on the fence watching the goats. Cody had to admit they really were funny. "I think they're the clowns of the farm," he said. His dad nodded his head in agreement.

Then they talked about the other farm animals — friendly dogs, squealy pigs, large cows, strong bulls, squawky chickens, cuddly kittens and lambs and the magnificent riding horse.

Cody was thinking about the tame farm animals and the wild animals that shared the farm. "I think it's great God made all the animals different," he said. "It's so much fun to watch them and learn about them."

Mr. Daniels agreed, "God gave us all these animals and hundreds more — just think of all the insects. But God didn't just want us to look at the animals or use them. He wants us to take care of them, too."

"Guess that means we keep fixing the fences," Cody said.

Your Turn

1. Why did God create animals?
2. How do animals help people?
3. How can you care for animals?

_____

_____

_____

Prayer

God, thanks for making all the wonderful animals. Help me to care for Your beautiful creation. Amen.

FARM ANIMALS AND FRIENDS

God must have had a great time creating all the different animals! Find the names of the animals hidden in this puzzle. The answers are on page 248.

Butterfly	Fish	Chicken	Chipmunk	Cow
Dog	Duck	Goat	Hawk	Horse
Kitten	Lamb	Meadowlark	Mosquito	Opossum
Rabbit	Raccoon	Rooster	Sheep	Squirrel
Swallow	Trout	Turtle		

Which of these animals would make a neat pet? _____

How would you take care of it? _____

_____

```
J E B E D S W A L L O W N
S Q U I R R E L A M B A O
M R T A L E H S I F T A O
E A T O N E T T I K N R C
A B E R O O S T E R C E C
D B R E N T R O U T H L A
O I F G T I K C U D I T R
W T L K N U M P I H C R T
L T Y C E Q D O G R K U A
A L L O L S H E E P E T O
R R A W H O R S E A N E G
K W A H D M U S S O P O W
```

LEARNING ABOUT GOD'S CREATION

God gave plants for me to use and enjoy.
The land was filled with seed-bearing plants and trees.
Genesis 1:12 NLT

Millions of Seeds

Old Mr. and Mrs. Bartlett sat on their back porch and smiled as they watched the activity swirling around them. Busy sounds were coming from all directions as the Junior High Youth Group weeded, mowed and trimmed their back yard. The leader, Mr. Carlson, directed the activity.

Todd and Jamal were weeding a large flower bed. Todd tugged and pulled at a stubborn weed. "These roots must be buried in concrete!" he said as he braced his feet and gave a mighty yank. As the weed gave way, Todd lost his balance and sprawled in the dirt.

Jamal cracked up laughing. "Hey, man, you are one messy dude," he teased, "sitting in a pile of dirt, sweat running down your nose and muddy streaks all over your face."

"You're not exactly Mr. Clean!" Todd shot back.

Just then Mr. Carlson called, "Take a break and cool off."

All the kids rushed to the porch to enjoy the lemonade and cookies Mr. and Mrs. Bartlett served. "This is just a little thank-you for all your hard work," Mrs. Bartlett said.

"The yard and flower beds do look pretty good, but sometimes I think I hate plants!" Todd announced.

"The world wouldn't survive very long without them," Mr. Carlson said. "They provide food for people and animals, clean the air, make oxygen, hold soil in place and keep us cool. They also give us products like lumber, medicines and paper."

Todd sighed. "I know you're right. But I wish the weeds would grow somewhere far away from flower beds and lawns."

Your Turn

1. Have you ever taken care of plants? What did you do?
2. Why do we need to protect plants?

Prayer

Lord, thank You for giving us so many plants. Even though they are work to take care of, they provide many important things for us. Amen.

BIBLE PLANTS

The Bible mentions many plants by name. Decode the words to find some of the plants. Use a New International Version (NIV) Bible. The answers are on page 248.

A	B	C	D	E	F	G	H	I	J	K	L	M
7	12	20	1	8	3	15	10	6	23	14	9	22

N	O	P	Q	R	S	T	U	V	W	X	Y	Z
17	4	19	24	18	13	21	2	5	11	26	16	25

_____ Psalm 17:8

7, 19, 19, 9, 8

_____ 1 Kings 5:6

20, 8, 1, 7, 18, 13

_____ John 12:24

11, 10, 8, 7, 21

_____2 Samuel 6:19

1, 7, 21, 8, 13

_____, _____ Numbers 13:23

19, 4, 22, 8, 15, 18, 7, 17, 7, 21, 8, 13   3, 6, 15, 13

_____ John 6:9

12, 7, 18, 9, 8, 16

_____ Deuteronomy 24:21

15, 18, 7, 19, 8, 13

_____ Song of Songs 2:1

18, 4, 13, 8

_____ Revelation 11:4

4, 9, 6, 5, 8

_____, _____, _____ Numbers 11:5

20, 2, 20, 2, 22, 12, 8, 18, 13   22, 8, 9, 4, 17, 13   4, 17, 6, 4, 17, 13

_____ Luke 12:27

9, 6, 9, 6, 8, 13

_____ Luke 13:19

22, 2, 13, 21, 7, 18, 1

LEARNING ABOUT GOD'S CREATION

There is always something to appreciate about God's creation. *The earth is the Lord's, and everything in it, the world, and all who live in it; for he founded it upon the seas and established it upon the waters.*

Psalm 24:1-2

Camping Trip

"Smell that fresh air." Mrs. Clark paused to take a deep breath.

"Uh-huh," Reggie mumbled as he played with his computer game. "Yeah!" he yelled afterward. "I got 15,000 points!"

Mrs. Clark shook her head. "Reg, the whole idea of this mother-son camping trip is to look at what God created. Please put the game down."

"Okay, okay. Just one second." Reggie was soon interested in what was happening on the tiny screen before him. Suddenly, the game was taken out of his hands. "Mooooommm, I was almost a war warrior! I only needed one more point."

"Look." Mrs. Clark waved at the scenery before them. The horizon seemed a million miles away beyond the crystal lake near their campsite.

"It is sort of neat," Reggie admitted. "Hey, look over there!" He watched as a kingfisher suddenly made a dive for the water, soon coming up with a fish. "Cool." His mother put her arm around him as she grabbed him in a quick hug.

"I think you're cool, too," she said.

Your Turn

1. What do you appreciate about God's creation?

_____

_____

2. How often do you stop to notice what's around you? (Circle one.)

Every day   Once or twice a week   Once a month   Never

Prayer

Lord, everything in Your creation points to how amazing You are. Amen.

LEARN ALL ABOUT IT

What do you want to learn about God's creation? How will you go about learning it? You could...

...check out a magazine like National Geographic or National Geographic World.

...check a book out of the library on animals or plants.

...check out creation around you by taking a walk.

...check out a film or TV show on the wonders of nature.

When you find some interesting facts,
don't forget to give God some praise!

LEARNING ABOUT GOD'S CREATION

Learning about creation helps me learn about God.
*God made two great lights — the greater light to govern the day
and the lesser light to govern the night.*

Genesis 1:16

Stars and Black Holes

Kyle Richards had been fascinated in science class that day. The teacher had talked about black holes in space and stars brighter than the sun. Kyle had a lot of information to tell his father when his dad arrived home from work that evening.

"Did you know that the sun is a small star compared to some others?" Kyle announced.

"Interesting," his father said.

"The sun is 846,000 miles in diameter. To think that God made that!" Kyle looked impressed.

Mr. Richards chuckled. "Well, God's a pretty big God. The sun's size is nothing compared to Him."

"Did you know that the gravity of a black hole pulls stuff into it? Light and stuff," Kyle continued. "Isn't that cool?"

"What's cool is that God is stronger than a black hole."

Kyle shrugged. "I hadn't realized that God was so big."

His father clapped a hand on his shoulder. "Son, you've just said more in that one statement than many adults learn in a lifetime."

Your Turn

1. What are some of the biggest things in creation?
2. What is the biggest animal or land forms that you've seen?
3. Since God made everything, even the things you can't see, do you think you can trust Him to solve your biggest problems? Why or why not?

_____

_____

_____

_____

_____

Prayer

Lord, when I look around at the world, I see Your hand everywhere. Amen.

BLACK HOLES AND STARS

Albert Einstein and Isaac Newton, who were both physicists, made discoveries that helped scientists find the black holes. Black holes are formed when a giant star "dies." The sun that our Earth orbits is a star, one of many in the Milky Way Galaxy. To escape the gravitational pull of a black hole, you would have to travel faster than the speed of light. Sounds scary! But just think, God is more powerful than that!

What problem or concern do you have right now that seems like a black hole — it seems to pull all of the energy out of you?

_____

_____

_____

Take a moment to pray about that concern. Ask God to help you see the light at the end of the tunnel—the hope He can provide.

CARING FOR GOD'S CREATION

God appointed me to take care of the Earth.
*The Lord God had formed out of the ground all the beasts of the
field and all the birds of the air. He brought them to the man to
see what he would name them.*

Genesis 2:15, LB

Someone to Care

Jennifer Brenner dropped the magazine on her brother's face as he lay on the couch watching TV.

"Hey!" Conor cried, brushing the magazine away.

Jennifer picked it up and pointed to an article. "You need to read this. This boy rescues sea turtles."

"So?" Conor said.

"So, he cares about animals. *Somebody* should." Jennifer looked hard at her brother.

"Mom, Jen's nagging me!" Conor called. "Can I hit her?"

"No!" their mom replied. "Jen, quit nagging your brother."

Conor settled for pushing his sister instead. She pushed him back. "He's been harming animals, Mom!" she announced.

Conor waved her away. "Just because I threw one pebble at a goose."

Jennifer sighed heavily. "You know you shouldn't hurt a harmless animal."

"Harmless? It hissed at me. I thought it was gonna bite me!"

"You looked like you were going to hurt her baby. She was only protecting it. Like we're supposed to protect what God made."

Conor silently mimicked her, then said, "So, whaddya want me to do? Say I'm sorry to the goose?"

"You should say you're sorry to God."

Your Turn

1. Do you agree with Jennifer? Why or why not?
2. What is harmful to God's creation?
3. God allowed Adam to name the animals. What responsibility do you think went along with naming the animals?

Prayer

Lord Jesus, everything You put under my care makes me aware of what I need to do to maintain it. Amen.

YOU'RE A MEMBER

Congratulations! You've been drafted into the WCAGC! Those letters stand for "We Care About God's Creation." Members of this group do more than talk about God's creation. They take an active part in caring for it. As a member, you can write your own rules of membership. Answer the questions below. Then design a WCAGC logo in the space provided below. Explain how your logo tells your views on caring about God's creation.

How would you care about God's creation?

_____

How would you recruit others to this cause?

_____

I designed this logo because:

_____

CARING FOR GOD'S CREATION

We can take care of God's creation in big and small ways.
*The Lord God placed the man in the Garden of
Eden as its gardener, to tend and care for it.*

Genesis 2:19

Caretakers of the Planet

Conor Brenner tossed the can toward the park's already overflowing garbage can. Instead of going in, it bounced off the rim onto the ground.

"Aren't you going to recycle that?" his sister Jennifer asked.

Conor rolled his eyes. "Here we go again! Another lecture about Creation! I'm sick of recycling! They only pay 29 cents a pound for cans. You can't make any money like that."

Jennifer put her hands on her hips, trying to look mature and stern. "Don't you care about the planet?"

Conor silently mimicked her, then said, "One little can isn't going to hurt the planet."

"It will if everybody thinks like you do."

"Who are you? Mother Nature?"

Jennifer gave him a look. "God says we're supposed to care about what He created. I'm just telling you." Jennifer grabbed the can. "Well, if you won't, I will."

Your Turn

1. What have you done to care for God's creation this week?
2. Do you think that caring for the environment is everyone's responsibility or the responsibility of a few? Why or why not?
3. God gave Adam the job of taking care of creation. That job was passed down to us. Why do you think God wants people to care for His creation?

_____

_____

_____

_____

Prayer

God, help me to be a considerate caretaker of Your creation. Amen.

CREATION CLOSEUPS

Can you tell what these natural items are by looking at each up close? If you need a hint, read each description. (You don't have to know the exact species, just a general name.) Looking at these items "larger than life" makes you realize that there is more to creation than meets the eye. God wants you to have eyes that see the value of His creation. The answer is on page 248.

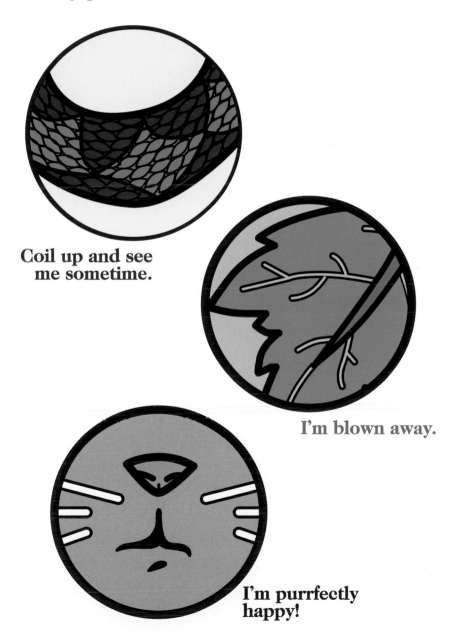

Coil up and see me sometime.

I'm blown away.

I'm purrfectly happy!

I CAN COOPERATE

WITH MY TALENTS AND GIFTS

Appreciating the abilities God has given
me helps me cooperate with others.
*There is no need for me to write to you about this service to the
saints. For I know your eagerness to help.*
2 Corinthians 9:1-2

Talent Talk

"You need a sand wedge for that," Marshall Albright suggested. Marshall and his brother were on the last hole of the nine-hole golf course.

"If I make the next two shots, I'll beat you by two strokes," Lawrence said. "You sure you want me to use a sand wedge? Unless you're trying to give me bad advice."

Lawrence knew that his younger brother's advice was good. Even though he was 12, Marshall was pretty good at golf. Lawrence, who was 15, only beat him occasionally now. He decided to take his advice. The ball sailed crisply out of the sand onto the green. One putt later, it was in the hole.

Marshall gave his brother a high-five as they joined their father in the clubhouse. "Who won?" he asked.

"I did," Lawrence said proudly. He got his younger brother in a headlock. "But I couldn't have done it without Marsh."

Marshall wriggled out of the headlock. He was pleased at his brother's words.

"I'm glad you're cooperating," their father said. He knew how competitive the boys were.

"I know I'm good," Marshall said. "That's why I can help those less fortunate." He grinned slyly at his brother.

Your Turn

1. What talents or abilities has God given you?
2. How will you use those talents to cooperate with others?

Prayer

Lord, whatever my gifts and abilities are, help me use them to help others and bring praise to Your name. Amen.

PAPER PINBALL 2

You played paper pinball on page 21. This time, to launch your first ball through the game, write on the lines below the ability or abilities that Joseph and David had. To launch your second ball through the game, write the names of the people they cooperated with through the use of their gifts. For each correct answer, you get 5 points. If you need a hint, look at Genesis 39:20-22; 40:8-10; 1 Samuel 16:15-21; 18:10. The answers are on page 248.

WITH MY TALENTS AND GIFTS

Love for others helps me cooperate with my abilities.
Dear children, let us not love with words
or tongue but with actions and in truth.

1 John 3:18

Helping Out of Love

"For the last time, no! I'm busy!" Dennis Allen shooed his younger brother away.

"But it'll only take you a second to show me how to fold the paper to make a puppet." Terrence looked at Dennis with pleading eyes.

"I've got to finish sweeping out the garage. Unless…I'll make you a deal. You do the sweeping and I'll make your puppet."

"Okay!" Terrence accepted the broom that Dennis offered.

"Oh, Dennis!" their father called.

"Oh boy." Dennis reluctantly went out into the yard, where their father was.

"Don't make your brother do your chores," Mr. Allen said.

"I wasn't making him. He wants me to help him. He can help me. That's cooperation," Dennis said. "Isn't that what you told me?"

"I know what cooperation means. It also means helping someone out of love, not out of what you can get that person to do. That's what I've been trying to get you to see."

Dennis shrugged. "Okay."

Your Turn

1. How could Dennis take his father's advice?
2. How could you use your abilities to help others out of love?
3. Why is that important?

_____

_____

_____

_____

_____

Prayer

Lord, show me how to cooperate with others. Amen.

ALL YOU NEED IS...WHAT?

One of the words in the Scripture at left will guide you through this maze. You have to find out which one, since you'll go through the maze letter by letter. Which word guided you through? Let that be a hint! The answer is on page 248.

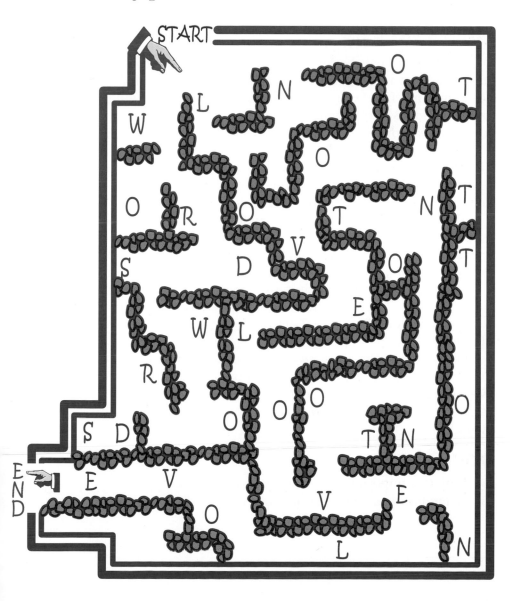

AT HOME

God wants me to be cooperative at home.
I appeal to you...that all of you agree with one another.
1 Corinthians 1:10

House for Sale

David looked at the for sale sign in the front yard. He felt both happy and sad about moving. He would miss the neighborhood and the big tree for climbing. But David was looking forward to having a room all to himself and he wouldn't have to change schools. Before David could think about it anymore, he heard his dad calling the family to the front yard.

"OK, troops," Mr. Johnson said. "We need to get this lawn in tip-top shape so people will want to stop and look at the house. Everyone choose your weapon." He pointed to the mower, wheelbarrow, trimmers, a big mound of top soil and several flats of colorful flowers.

David looked around at the long grass, the overgrown bushes and the weedy flower beds. "Oh, yuck, this yard's a mess. It will take forever to make it look great," David replied. His sister Erica just rolled her eyes and gave a big sigh.

"If everyone works together, we can get it in great shape. You kids can start by pulling the weeds in the flower beds. Start in the front and work your way around the house. Let's get to it," Mr. Johnson said as he started the mower.

By Sunday night, after a weekend of hard work and some complaining, the yard was all ready for interested buyers. As David rubbed the calluses on his hands he said, "I hope the people at our new house are getting that yard in 'tip-top shape' too. I don't think I want to do this again for a while!"

Your Turn

1. Why is it important for a family to cooperate?
2. What are the advantages of cooperating?

Prayer

Lord, help me to cooperate with my family members. I know it is how You want me to behave, but it can be difficult. Amen.

WORKING TOGETHER

Cooperation means working together to get something done. Use the code to figure out some people that need to cooperate. The answer is on page 248.

CODE

A	B	C	D	E	F	G	H	I	J	K	L	M
26	25	24	23	22	21	20	19	18	17	16	15	14

N	O	P	Q	R	S	T	U	V	W	X	Y	Z
13	12	11	10	9	8	7	6	5	4	3	2	1

8 11 12 9 7 7 22 26 14 8

24 19 6 9 24 19   14 22 14 25 22 9 8

22 14 11 15 12 2 22 22 8

21 18 9 22 21 18 20 19 7 22 9 8

26 9 14 2

12 9 24 19 22 8 7 9 26

21 26 14 18 15 2

8 7 6 23 22 13 7 8

COOPERATION AT HOME

God likes a family that cooperates.
How good and pleasant it is when brothers live together in unity.
Psalm 133:1

Unfinished Business

It was a beautiful fall day — and it was Saturday. *Perfect football weather,* thought Bob as he hurried through his breakfast. Bob tucked the football under his arm and headed to the garage to get his bike. Bob's father was in the garage looking around.

"Bob, your job for this week was to clean out the garage. Well, you still have today to do it."

"Oh, Dad. It's such a great day and I'm meeting the guys at the park to play some football. It will take all day to get this garage in shape," Bob complained. "I promise I'll do it tomorrow."

Mr. Tucker shook his head and said, "No, way. You already wasted the whole week — and it was your job. This is unfinished business with a deadline of today."

Bob sighed and kicked the garbage can. He sighed again as he started to work on a stack of newspapers. His dad heard all the heavy sighing and saw the grouchy look on Bob's face. He said, "In a family, each person needs to do his or her part. We need to work together — that's called cooperation. Why don't you start working right now instead of complaining. You can probably finish before the day is over."

Bob moved a little faster as he thought of playing a late afternoon football game.

Your Turn

1. Why is family cooperation so important?
2. What jobs do you have in your family?

_____

_____

_____

_____

_____

Prayer

Dear God, help our family work together in unity. Amen.

LIVING IN UNITY

Figure out the clues, and write the answers on the blank. The answers are on page 248.

— — —   — — —   . . .   — — — —   — — —
  1   5   4   12

— — — —   — —   — — — — — — —
  14   3   7

— — — — — —   — — — —   — — —
   13   8   2

— — — — .   — — — — —   — —:—
   10   6   9 11

1. Fifth month of the year

2. Another word for "one" (rhymes with "peach")

3. Opposite of "out"

4. What you say when you're in trouble

5. Rhymes with "rod"

6. Sixth book in the New Testament

7. Opposite of "incomplete"

8. Add a "w" to the front of "it" and an "h" to the end

9. Number of disciples plus three

10. Rhymes with "mother"

11. 10-5

12. Opposite of "me"

13. Add "ony" to the end of a word that means "hurt"

14. Replace the "f" in "five" with an "L"

COOPERATION AT SCHOOL

I am to cooperate with everyone, not just those I like.
God does not show favoritism, but accepts men from every
nation who fear him and do what is right.

Acts 10:34b-35

Help in Time of Need

"Uh, can I call you back? Someone's on the other line." Mark Gleason clicked the cordless phone back to his friend Keith. "As I was saying…"

"Was that Karen again?" Keith asked.

"Yeah." Mark made a face. "Ever since the teacher put her in my math study group, she's been asking me for help. I wish she wouldn't bug me."

Keith laughed. "I think she likes you."

"Ugh. Why couldn't it be Katy Shepherd? She's cute. I'd help her any day." Katy Shepherd was the best looking girl in the sixth grade.

"Mark, listen to yourself," his older brother Lance interrupted from the family room. "You're not gonna help the girl just because you don't like her?"

"I'm on the phone!" Mark yelled.

"So? As loud as you talk I can't help but hear."

"Mom! Make Lance leave me alone!" Mark called.

"I agree with Lance," their mother replied.

"I'm going to my room!" Mark huffed. He didn't want to admit that they were both right.

Your Turn

1. What are some ways you can be cooperative with kids from school?
2. With whom do you find it hardest to be cooperative? Why?
3. Why is it important to cooperate with all kinds of people, not just those you like?

Prayer

Lord, sometimes I don't want to be cooperative, especially with people I have a hard time liking. Show me how to get along with all kinds of people. Amen.

COOPERATIVE ATTITUDES

Use the code to figure out words that describe cooperative attitudes. But watch out! You'll have to hunt, because the alphabet isn't exactly in order. The answer is on page 248.

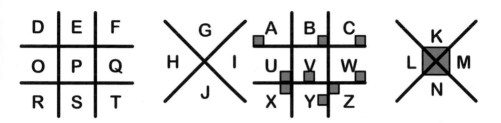

1.

2.

to help

3.

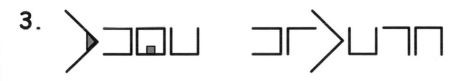

COOPERATION AT SCHOOL

Love for Jesus helps me cooperate with others.
If anyone is in Christ, he is a new creation;
the old has gone, the new has come!

2 Corinthians 5:17

Operation Cooperation

The mud puddle looked so inviting. And Mallory Branford, the biggest know-it-all in the fifth grade, was close to it. Justin Porter longed to stick out his foot as Mallory walked past. Splat! She'd fall right in the mud puddle. Oh, it would be sweet. Instead...

"You serve like this." Justin smacked the volleyball with his fist. It sailed across to his friend Peter, who spiked it just as another girl reached for it.

"Oh," Mallory said. "That's what I've been doing wrong."

The gym teacher blew the whistle to call everyone back inside the school. Peter caught up to Justin as they headed in. "Why were you helping her?" he asked Justin. "I thought you couldn't stand her."

Justin shrugged. "She doesn't bother me as much as she used to."

Peter stared at him. "Who are you and what have you done with my best friend?"

Justin laughed. "I'm just trying to...y'know do what God wants for a change." He looked slightly embarrassed.

"You have changed since you became a Christian, as you said," Peter said. "There must be something more to God than I thought."

Your Turn

1. Why did Justin help Mallory?
2. How does Jesus help you cooperate with others?

_____

_____

_____

_____

Prayer

Dear God, show me ways to cooperate with others, like Jesus did. Amen.

MY CARD

Many professionals carry business cards that share their experience. When a professional hands out a card, that's his or her way of telling someone, "I'm willing to work with you." What would you put on a business card to show kids at your school that you're willing to be cooperative? Use the card below to write what you would put on your card. Choose a snappy, attention-getting logo and a slogan to go on your card. (See example below.)

COOPERATION AT CHURCH

I can show thanks to God by cooperating with others.
*Whatever you do, whether in word or deed, do it all in the name
of the Lord Jesus, giving thanks to God the Father through him.*
Colossians 3:17

Doug's Turn

It was Doug's turn to pray at dinner. "Thank You, God, for giving us this food and all You do for us," he prayed. "Amen." A millisecond after the prayer, he said, "Pass the pork chops."

"Are you really thankful to God?" his father asked.

"About the pork chops? Yeah!" Doug loved pork chop night.

His father threw him a measuring look. "About anything."

Doug looked puzzled. "What do you mean, Dad?"

His father passed the pork chops. "I've been getting reports that you and your friends were the ones making a lot of noise last week after youth church ended."

Doug quickly grabbed two chops. "We were just messing around in the gym. We didn't think anyone could hear us."

"I heard him, too!" Benjie, the youngest, said.

"Nobody asked you!" Doug said.

"Well, you know the adult service sometimes runs a little long. If you disturb others, that cuts into their ability to worship God. Cooperating with others is the best way to say thanks to God."

Your Turn

1. How could Doug have been more cooperative?
2. How does cooperation help you show thanks to God?

_____

_____

_____

_____

_____

Prayer

Lord, I want to show my thanks to You by thinking of others and helping them in any way that I can. Amen.

YOUR OFFERING OF THANKS

To remind you of the memory verse above, search for the red words in the puzzle below. The answer is on page 248.

Remember:

Whatever you do, **whether** in **word** or **deed**, do it **all** in the **name** of the **Lord Jesus**, giving **thanks** to **God** the **Father through him.**

~ Colossians 3:17

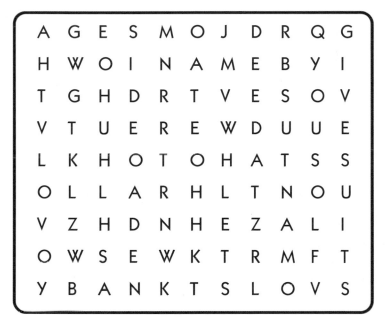

```
A G E S M O J D R Q G
H W O I N A M E B Y I
T G H D R T V E S O V
V T U E R E W D U U E
L K H O T O H A T S S
O L L A R H L T N O U
V Z H D N H E Z A L I
O W S E W K T R M F T
Y B A N K T S L O V S
```

COOPERATING AT CHURCH

Cooperating at church helps everyone worship God.
Show proper respect to everyone:
Love the brotherhood of believers.

1 Peter 2:17a

Volunteers, Anyone?

"We need some volunteers to help out in the nursery," Mr. Philips said. "Just for one Sunday."

Lloyd Mason half listened to his Sunday school teacher. He wasn't about to volunteer.

"Why do we have to do this?" one girl asked.

"Another church is visiting ours," Mr. Philips said. "That means a lot of small children will be here. Taking care of their children will allow their parents to worship."

"Yeah, but that means we'll miss youth church," one boy brought up.

"It's a sacrifice," Mr. Philips replied. "That's why I'm asking for volunteers. How 'bout you, Lloyd?"

Lloyd snorted. Hold some drooling babies? No way.

"Come on. I've been bragging to everyone about how cooperative and mature my fifth and sixth grade class is. This is a way to show that you worship God, too."

"How? We'll miss church," Lloyd said.

"God honors any sacrifice made on behalf of someone else. Helping their parents worship is an act of worship, too."

"Well…" Lloyd considered. "As long as I'm not the only one doing it."

Mr. Philips smiled. "Don't worry. I've just decided that my whole class will help out. We all need a lesson in cooperation."

Your Turn

1. What are some jobs at your church that require cooperation?
2. What are some things you can do to help others worship?

_____

_____

_____

Prayer

Lord, I want to cooperate with the people within my church family, not because I'm supposed to, but because I want to. Amen.

CHURCH COOPERATION

You've been picked to report on church cooperation. When the church first started, there was plenty of cooperation! Acts 2:41-47 is your beat. Your job as a reporter is to find out who, what, when, where, why and how. The answers are on page 248.

REPORT

1. **Who cooperated?**
   (See verse 41) _____
   _____
   _____

2. **How did they cooperate?**
   (See verses 42, 44, and 46) _____
   _____
   _____

3. **What did they use to help each other?**
   (See verse 45) _____
   _____
   _____

4. **When did they meet?**
   (See verse 46) _____
   _____
   _____

5. **Why did they cooperate with each other?**
   (See verses 43 and 47) _____
   _____
   _____

Bonus Question: How do the people within your church congregation cooperate with each other? _____
_____
_____

WHAT DOES GOD SAY ABOUT...

MONEY

God wants me to make wise decisions about money.
Let no debt remain outstanding, except the
continuing debt to love one another.

Romans 13:8a

A Wise Move

"Ooo." Erick Rather practically shoved his nose through the window as he stopped to check out the display. "They've got the new War Zone game," he told his old brother Todd.

"I know you're not thinking about buying it. You owe me $5," Todd said.

"I'll pay you back later. Besides, you're loaded. Didn't you just get paid from your after-school job?"

"What's that got to do with the fact that you owe me money?"

Erick tried his best to look pitiful. "You should feel sorry for me. I have to get by on allowance."

"I don't feel sorry for you. Pay up, if you've got the money."

"I could hear you two arguing all the way at the end of the mall," their mother said, as she came down the mall corridor. "What is it now?"

"He won't give me the $5 he owes me," Todd announced.

"I don't want you boys fighting over money."

"Mom, can you loan me $5 to pay back Todd, then?" Erick asked. "I want to buy this game with my birthday money. You said I could."

"That was before I learned you owe Todd money. Now, what's the wise thing to do when you owe someone money and you have it?"

Erick grinned. "Uh, beg that person to wait a little while longer?"

"Nice try."

Your Turn

1. What was Erick's first responsibility, rather than buying the game?
2. Why is it important to pay people you owe?

_____

_____

_____

Prayer

Lord, show me how to be wise about money. Amen.

MONEY MANAGER

Play this game by yourself or with a friend to practice making wise decisions with money. You start off with $30. You'll need paper and pencil or a calculator to keep track of your money. Flip a coin to move. Heads = move one space; tails = move two spaces. If you play with a friend, flip a coin to see who goes first. (Heads = second; tails = first.) At the end of the game, see who has made the wisest decisions by keeping out of debt.

MONEY

God wants me to wisely consider
my reasons for acquiring more money.
*Be...as God wants you to be; not greedy
for money, but eager to serve.*

1 Peter 5:2

Money Matters

"Put down 'Kids growing up in the new millennium need more allowance money,' " Erick Rather told his friend Sean.

Erick and Sean were at Sean's house writing a note demanding more allowance. Both boys planned to present a copy to their parents.

"Hey, that's good. We should also say that we have more responsibilities and need more money," Sean suggested.

"Why do you want more money?" Erick asked.

"I just want to have more than Kris Fiedler. She's always bragging about how much she gets."

"I just want more period. I spend all of mine too quickly."

The boys made two copies, then agreed to meet again in two days to see how their plan worked.

"What'd your mom say?" Sean asked, when he saw Erick's glum face.

"She laughed at first. Then she said stuff about God and my not giving her a good reason for wanting more money."

"My dad told me to do more chores if I wanted more money." Sean didn't look as if he thought that were a good idea.

"Maybe we shouldn't have written the stuff about having more responsibilities."

After sitting in silence for a minute, Erick came to a decision. "Maybe...we need to take their advice."

Your Turn

1. Why did Erick want more allowance? What was Sean's reason? In your opinion, did they both have good reasons? Why or why not?

2. How do people fall into the habit of worshipping money, rather than God? How can this be avoided?

Prayer

Lord, help me worship You, instead of money. Amen.

THE PRICE IS RIGHT?

Money was used for better or worse in the Bible. Choose the amount that answers each question. Give yourself 25 points for each correct answer. The answers are on page 248.

1. How much was Judas paid to betray Jesus? (Matthew 26:14-16)

   a. 10 shekels of silver   b. 20 shekels of silver   c. 30 shekels of silver

2. How much were Joseph's brothers paid for selling him? (Genesis 37:28)

   a. 10 shekels of silver   b. 20 shekels of silver
   c. 30 shekels of silver

3. How much did Abraham pay for a family tomb? (Genesis 23:14-16)

   a. 200 shekels of silver b. 400 shekels of silver c. 600 shekels of silver

4. How much did Jesus and the disciples notice that the widow put into the offering? (Mark 12:41-44)

   a. 2 copper coins   b. 1 silver coin   c. 10 copper coins

5. Jesus told a parable about a king who gave his servants a specific amount of talents (money). How much did the person who was given five talents earn? (Matthew 25:19-20)

   a. 5 more talents   b. 10 more talents c. 15 more talents

6. How many pieces of silver did the woman in Jesus' parable about the lost coin have before she lost the coin? (Luke 15:8-10)

   a. 5   b. 10   c. 15

7. How much was the coin in the fish's mouth worth? (Matthew 17:27)

   a. 2 denarii   b. 2 drachmas   c. 4 drachmas

RESPECTING ADULTS

God wants me to respect adults, especially the elderly.
Rise in the presence of the aged, show respect
for the elderly and revere your God. I am the Lord.
Leviticus 19:32

Always Around

Desmond and his friend Alex pushed his way through the crowd of mall shoppers. They almost knocked over an elderly woman who slowly made her way down the mall.

"Watch it!" the woman said.

"All these old, crabby people!" Alex grumbled loud enough to be overheard by the elderly woman. They continued walking. "If they can't walk fast, why don't they stay at home?"

Desmond suddenly regretted not having said "Excuse me" to the woman. He knew his father would have been disappointed in the way he had treated her. *But he's not here,* he argued with himself. Yet he knew his heavenly Father is always around.

"Wait a sec," he told Alex. He ran back to the woman. "I'm sorry we pushed you," he said.

The woman looked surprised to see him again. "That's all right," she said.

Alex shook his head at him when he returned. "Why'd you bother?" he asked.

Desmond shrugged. "I was thinking about my Father."

Your Turn

1. How did Desmond show respect?
2. How do you show respect for those older than you?
3. Why is it important to show respect for adults?

_____

_____

_____

_____

_____

Prayer

Lord, show me how to be respectful to the adults in my life. Amen.

RESPECT BINGO

This is a game where everyone is a winner — you and the people with whom you come into contact. Play this with a brother or sister or with a friend. This game will take some time — you can't do it all in one day. You both can choose a square. For the free square, write in the person of your choice. Each time you show respect for one of the people listed below, place your initials on the square. The first person to get three in a row gets to call out "Bingo."

BINGO

Mom	Dad	Aunt or Uncle
Grand-parent	A Teacher	Grand-parent
A Teacher	Free Square	Neighbor

BINGO

Mom	Dad	Aunt or Uncle
Grand-parent	A Teacher	Grand-parent
A Teacher	Free Square	Neighbor

RESPECTING ADULTS

Respect for adults gains me respect.

*Obey [your leaders] so that their work will be a joy, not a burden,
for that would be of no advantage to you.*

Hebrews 13:17b

Respect + Respect = Respect

"I need you guys to be quiet while the announcements are read," Amy, one of the youth pastors announced.

Jason noticed how tired she looked. "What's with Amy?" he whispered to his friend Simon.

"I heard she's ready to quit," Simon replied. "Some of the kids have been mouthing off to her. You know, not showing her any respect."

The youth group had already lost one of the three youth pastors they'd had. Jason remembered hearing his parents talking about it.

He didn't want Amy to go. She seemed to really love the kids in the group. As he glanced around the auditorium, he noticed how some of the kids continued talking while Amy read the announcements. He suddenly got up, put two fingers in his mouth and whistled loudly. "You guys!" he cried after everyone was silent. "Didn't you hear Amy ask for quiet?"

"Thank you, Jason," Amy said. After the youth group meeting, she said, "That was a big help to me, Jason. I've been thinking about...making some changes to make my job a little easier. I've decided to choose some of you to be group leaders. I respect your judgment. I think you'd make a good group leader. What do you say?"

Jason grinned in reply.

Your Turn

1. How did Jason earn respect?
2. How are you helped when you respect adults?

_____

_____

_____

_____

Prayer

Lord, I'm responsible for showing respect to _____ (fill in the name of an adult). Show me what to do and say. Amen.

RESPECT IS RIGHT

Have you ever heard your parents say, "Because I said so" when you asked them why you had to do something they wanted you to do? God sometimes responds that way when we ask Him why we need to obey Him. Respecting adults is one way to obey God. Why? Because He says so. How would the advice of the following verses help you respect these individuals? How can you gain respect in the process? Use the letter next to the verse to make a choice. The answers are on page 248.

1   **2**   **3**

1. Coach Franklin, who likes to tease kids who aren't very athletic
2. A parent who wants you to do chores you hate to do
3. A neighbor who wants you to do chores for her for little money

A. Honor your father and your mother. (Exodus 20:12)
B. Obey your leaders and submit to their authority. (Hebrews 13:17a)
C. Rise in the presence of the aged, show respect for the elderly and revere your God. I am the Lord. (Leviticus 19:32)
D. Show proper respect to everyone. (1 Peter 2:17)
E. The worker deserves his wages. (1 Timothy 5:18b)

1. I would use verse _____ because _____

_____

2. I would use verse _____ because _____

_____

3. I would use verse _____ because _____

_____

POPULARITY

I should be popular in a way that pleases God.
A friend loves at all times.

Proverbs 17:17

The "In" Crowd

Cal and Henry heard Jim Hanson and his buddies before they saw them. They were hanging out in a corner of the gym, laughing and goofing around. This group of sixth-grade boys was the coolest. They had all of the popular computer games and knew how to win at them. They knew the latest "in" words and jokes. These boys always did things together.

Cal gave a sigh as he tied his gym shoes. Then he asked Henry, "Wouldn't you like to be friends with Jim Hanson and the rest of his crowd?"

"I'm not sure," Henry replied.

One day after gym class, one of the group, Mike, sauntered over to Cal. Mike had a conversation with Cal as they walked to the classroom. Then Mike said, "How about playing football with us after school today?"

Cal almost tripped over his feet but he did manage to mutter, "Sure."

They played every day for a week. The games were rough and tumble, but Cal thought it was great to be part of the "in" crowd.

"Can you do something special for us?" Mike asked on Friday.

Cal's stomach did a flip-flop but he asked, "Like what?"

"We're playing some guys from Wiley School tomorrow. We can't stand them and we want to beat them any way we can. You're the biggest guy, so tackle them super hard and then give them an extra punch when they're down." Mike smacked his fist into his other hand.

Cal shook his head and said, "I can't do that. It's not playing fair."

"What a jerk! I knew you didn't belong in our group," Mike said as he stomped off.

Cal actually felt relieved. "They really aren't so cool after all," he told Henry later. "You're cooler because you're a real friend."

Your Turn

1. What makes someone popular in your school?
2. Are all those things God-pleasing? Why or why not?

Prayer

Heavenly Father, thank You for true friends who are always loyal. Amen.

GOD'S POPULARITY CONTEST

If God were having a popularity contest, what would He look for? You can shine like a star when you act in these ways. Cross out the G's, M's, Q's and W's to find out what they are. The answers are on page 248.

POPULARITY

God wants me to be myself.

I have learned to be content whatever the circumstances.

Philippians 4:11

The Chameleon Kid

Nate loved baseball. He read the newspaper sports every day, watched sports on TV and collected sports cards. He also played sports. He was the shortstop on the traveling baseball team, which was made up of the best players from all of the teams in the town league.

One Saturday morning, Nate's Uncle Steve called to ask for directions to the ball field because he wanted to see Nate play. "All right!" said Nate. "Wait until he sees how good our team plays. Will he be impressed!"

Nate saw his uncle, but he didn't want to look like a geek and wave to him, so he just nodded. The game was close with the lead changing several times. Along with hitting, fielding and pitching, there were arguments and angry outbursts. Nate's team finally squeaked out a win by one run.

Nate ran up to Uncle Steve and gave him a high five. Uncle Steve said, "I'm happy your team won but I'm disappointed in you." Nate could hardly believe his ears! He'd hit in two runs and made some great catches at center field.

Then his uncle continued, "Your playing was very good, but your actions were very poor. I saw you argue with the umpire, throw your bat when you were called out and use bad language."

"Everyone does those things. I don't see anything wrong with it. Do you want the other guys to think I'm a geek?" asked Nate.

"No, you're more like a chameleon," said Uncle Steve. "Chameleons change color to match their surroundings. You change your behavior to match the people you're with. How you act is very important to God and to people. When you're fair, cooperative and honest, other people will respect you."

Nate was quiet as he rode home with Uncle Steve.

Your Turn

1. How important is being one of the group?
2. What, if anything, do you do to make yourself fit in?

Prayer

Dear God, help me to act and speak in a way that is pleasing to You. Amen.

HOW ABOUT YOU?

Are you ever like a chameleon — changing to fit in with the crowd? Read the following statements and mark the box that best describes you.

	Usually	Sometimes	Never
1. I use bad language because the kids I'm with talk that way.			
2. I laugh at things that aren't really funny because everyone else is laughing.			
3. I won't be friends with some kids because they aren't very popular.			
4. When someone starts to talk about church or God, I change the subject.			
5. I tell little lies to make myself seem more important.			
6. I go along with my friends when they want me to do something wrong.			

PLANNING FOR THE FUTURE

God helps me plan for the future.

"For I know the plans I have for you," declares the Lord, "plans to prosper you and not to harm you, plans to give you hope and a future."

Jeremiah 29:11

Career Day

Career Day was in full swing in Aaron Barker's sixth-grade class.

"What are you doing now to prepare for the future?" one speaker asked the class.

One boy raised his hand. "I'm gonna be a rock musician," he said. "My dad just got me a new guitar."

"If that's what you want to do, what are you doing now to prepare for that career?"

The boy shrugged his shoulders. "I dunno. My dad won't let me play the guitar much. He says it's too loud."

"I'm gonna play in the NBA," another boy said. "They make a lot of money."

Aaron listened while everyone gave their plans. He wasn't sure what he wanted to do.

"What's up?" his mom asked when he arrived home.

"I'm not sure what I want to do in the future," he said. "There's a lot to think about. Where should I go to college? What kind of job should I have?"

"It's good to think about that now so you can begin to prepare," his mother said. "But it's not something for you to worry about. Don't forget. You can always ask God for help."

Your Turn

1. What are your plans for the future?
2. What plans do you think God has for you?

_____

_____

_____

_____

Prayer

Lord, show me the plans You have for my life. Amen.

ODD ONE OUT

Which of the items in each category does not belong? It's up to you to figure out which name or place doesn't belong in each category. The answers are on page 248.

- Disciples of Jesus (part of the 12): Matthew, Mark, Luke

- Women who knew Jesus while He was on earth: Mary, Martha, Lydia

- **People who traveled** with Paul on missionary journeys: Barnabas, Joshua, Silas

- **Your future plans:** driver's license, dating, college, marriage, fear

If you're wondering about the last category, read John 17:11, 17-19, 20-26. Jesus prayed for His disciples. He knew they'd need help to face the future. He even prayed for the believers who weren't even born yet! That includes you! What words of comfort does Jesus offer?

_____

_____

_____

PLANNING FOR THE FUTURE

God wants me to pray about the future.
Do not be anxious about anything, but in everything, by prayer and petition, with thanksgiving, present your requests to God.
Philippians 4:6

Future Fears

"Think the earth will blow up someday?" James asked his friend Chan as they left the movie theater.

Chan shrugged. His mind was still on the disaster movie they had just seen. The earth had been destroyed by a series of horrible disasters. He couldn't help feeling a little worried about the future. What if something like that happened?

The two boys were quiet as they climbed into Chan's brother's car. "What's up with you two?" he asked.

"We just saw *Time Disaster,*" Chan said.

"I saw that." His brother didn't look impressed.

"Do you think the stuff that happened in the movie could really happen?" Chan asked.

"Are you worried about that?"

"Promise you won't laugh?…Yeah."

He was glad that his brother kept his promise. "If you're worried about anything about the future, why not pray about it? See what God says about it. He cares about our futures too, y'know."

Your Turn

1. What are your fears concerning the future?
2. God cares about your future. What would you like to pray about now, concerning the future?

_____

_____

_____

_____

Prayer

Lord, I can't imagine the future without You. Guide me in the way that You would have me go. Amen.

FUTURE FEARS

Sometimes the future seems like a big, scary unknown. Thinking about changes in store can be like that. But there's one thing about the future that will never change. To find out what that is, use the dates in the code. The answers are on page 248.

CODE KEY

A	B	C	D	E	F	G	H	I	J	K	L	M
1910	2000	1954	1879	2010	864	1311	1785	1776	411	30	70	1902

N	O	P	Q	R	S	T	U	V	W	X	Y	Z
1999	1620	1948	1515	1865	702	2005	432	1011	1947	1500	1832	1212

411 2010 702 432 702

___ ___ ___ ___ ___

1954 1785 1865 1776 702 2005

___ ___ ___ ___ ___ ___

1776 702

___ ___

2005 1785 2010

___ ___ ___

702 1910 1902 2010

___ ___ ___ ___

1832 2010 702 2005 2010 1865 1879 1910 1832

___ ___ ___ ___ ___ ___ ___ ___ ___

1910 1999 1879

___ ___ ___

2005 1620 1879 1910 1832

___ ___ ___ ___ ___

1910 1999 1879

___ ___ ___

864 1620 1865 2010 1011 2010 1865

___ ___ ___ ___ ___ ___ ___ . ~ Hebrews 13:8

PLANNING FOR THE FUTURE

Everything about my past, present, and future is in God's hands. *We can make our plans, but the final outcome is in God's hands.*

Proverbs 16:1 LB

Going My Way?

Samuel Alexander's Sunday school class had just finished a Bible study on the apostle Paul's missionary journeys.

"Suppose God called you to be a missionary," his teacher said.

No way, Samuel thought. *I want to go to college and make a zillion dollars.*

"What if you don't want to be a missionary?" a girl asked. "Does God force you to do stuff?"

"God wants you to obey Him," the teacher replied. "He doesn't force you to do so, however."

"If God expects us to just do what He wants, what's the point of our making plans then?" Samuel asked.

"Because He never said you can't make plans," the teacher replied. "God wants you to trust Him with the future. He doesn't expect you to sit around doing nothing. But if you say you want Him to be Lord of your life, and you're serious about it, He does want some say about what you do. He wants us to trust Him enough to put our plans for the future in His hands."

Okay, God, Samuel thought. *I sure hope You want me to go to college and make a zillion dollars!*

Your Turn

1. What were Samuel's plans for the future? How willing do you think he was to allow God to lead him?
2. Suppose God's plans and your plans did not match. Whose plans would you follow? Why?

_____

_____

_____

Prayer

Lord, You are eternal. There's nothing about my present that You don't know. There's nothing about the future that You don't know. May all my plans give You glory. Amen.

TO INFINITY AND BEYOND!

Where will your plans for the future take you someday? Fill in this time line. What do you see yourself doing in one month? One year? Five years? Ten years? Here's your opportunity to make some concrete plans. Remember, although your plans may be concrete, nothing is "set in stone." Things change. God wants some say in what you do. Write your plans in the boxes below.

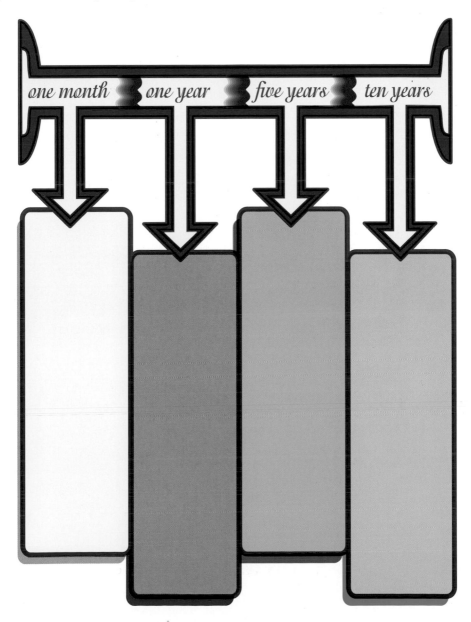

ANSWER KEY

page 13

page 17

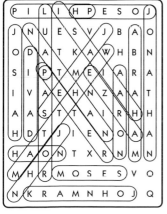

page 19

page 21
Prophets: Elijah, Elisha, Jeremiah, Miriam, Deborah
People who did miraculous things: Peter, Elijah, Elisha
Person who doesn't fit either category: Absalom (David's son)

page 23

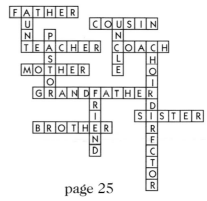

page 25

page 27

ANSWER KEY

page 29
1(c); 2(a); 3(b); 4(c); 5(a); 6(b);
7(c); 8(b); 9(b)

page 33
Put your trust in God.

page 35
The Lord will be with you.

page 37
A fool gives full vent to his anger,
but a wise man keeps himself
under control. Proverbs 29:11

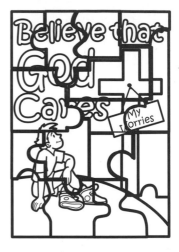

page 47

page 49
Trust in Your word (Psalm 119:42)

page 51
Four: God is 4 (for) you

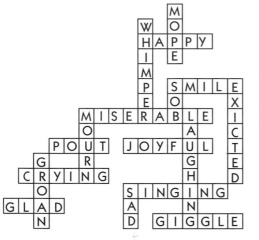

page 43

page 45
Philippians 4:6-7 could be used for
any of the worries. Other choices:
The future: Matthew 6:34;
death: John 11:25-26;
divorce: Philippians 4:6-7;
bad grades: Psalm 32:8

page 55

ANSWER KEY

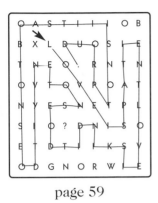

page 59

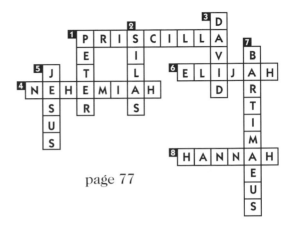

page 77

page 65

page 67
1. Joy in sorrow
2. Help is on the way
3. Beside yourself with joy
Bonus: Take (or accept) the good with the bad

page 75
Golden Hammer Award:
Noah (for building the ark)
Try-Try-Again Award:
Moses (asking for the Israelites' freedom)

page 81
Accept His Son, Jesus.

page 83
Trust in the Lord with all your heart. Proverbs 3:5

page 87
1. Ruth; 2. Jonathan; 3. Jesus

page 89
Peter, Joseph, Lot, Paul, ruthless

page 91
Ananias and Sapphira sold some land and gave the money to the apostles. Ananias and his wife kept part of the money but still claimed that they gave all that they had received. But Peter knew that Ananias had lied to the Holy Spirit about the amount of money he had received for the land. Because of that, Ananias died instantly! When his wife arrived, she was asked how much money they received. She gave the same answer that her husband did. Because of that, she died too! Everyone was terrified!

page 95
goats, donkey, ox, ostrich, stork, horse, hawk, eagle

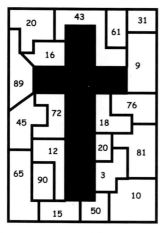

page 101

page 103
Ask your heavenly father for help.
Know His Word.

page 111
Do not lie. Do not deceive one another (Leviticus 19:11).

page 113
The top boy could say something like, "I forgive you." The bottom boy could say, "Sure. I'll help you."

page 115
The apple tree has one orange; the bird is upside-down; the sun and the moon are out at the same time; the dog has only three legs; one boy has one pant leg up; one boy is missing a shoe; a plate and fork are on the grass; the boy is telling the other boy that he doesn't forgive him (this is the main thing that is wrong!). The one thing that could be changed is the boy's speech balloon to "I forgive you."

page 117
1: Joseph's father, Jacob, gave him a special coat, which led to his brothers' jealousy.
2: After being sold into slavery, Joseph was in trouble again. His master had him thrown in prison.
3: Joseph, now the second-in-command in Egypt, forgave his brothers, who had come to him to buy grain.

page 123
Gideon/Menace to a horde of Midianites.
Deborah/Sacker of Sisera's army.
Samson/The Philistine foe.

page 125
Call to me and I will answer you. (Jeremiah 33:3)

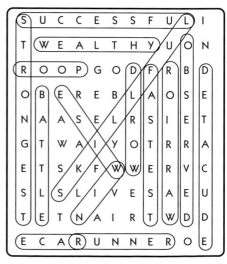

page 127

ANSWER KEY

page 139
Love, Trust, Peace, Cooperation

page 143
You are my friends if you do what I command. (John 15:14)

page 145
Yet to all who received him...he gave the right to become children of God. (John 1:12)

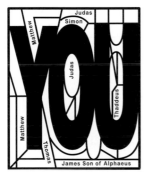

page 147

page 149
sinners, taxmen, deaf, lame, lepers, blind, poor, sick, insane

page 151
HUNGRY; FED; THIRSTY; DRINK; STRANGER; INVITED; HOME; NAKED; CLOTHING; SICK; CARED; PRISON; VISITED

page 159
Ask and it will be given to you; seek and you will find.
Matthew 7:7

page 163
I have hidden Your Word in my heart that I might not sin against You. (Psalm 119:11)

page 165
All Scripture is God-breathed.

page 167
1. The temple; Solomon; Collect cedar...
2. The ark; Noah; Collect cypress...
3. The tabernacle; Moses; Aaron; Collect 11 curtains...

page 169
I am the first and I am the last; apart from me there is no God. Who then is like me? (Isaiah 44:6)

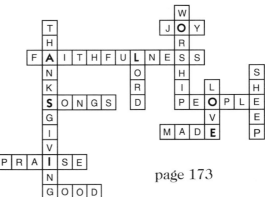

page 173

page 181
love, joy, peace, patience, kindness, goodness, faithfulness, gentleness, self-control.
You'll need patience as God works.

page 183
We have the mind of Christ.

page 185
1. respect; 2. time; 3. love; 4. help

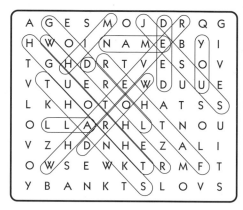

page 193

page 195
apple, cedars, wheat, dates, pomegranates, figs, barley, grapes, rose, olive, cucumbers, melons, onions, lilies, mustard

page 203
snake, leaf, cat

page 207
Joseph could interpret dreams and had leadership ability. He was in charge of running the prison for the jailer and cooperated with Pharaoh and Pharaoh's baker by interpreting their dreams. David could play the harp, which he used to soothe Saul.

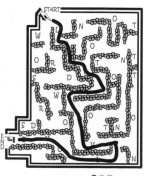

page 209

page 211
sport teams, church members, employees, firefighters, army, orchestra, family, students

page 213
May God...help you live in complete harmony with each other. Romans 15:5

page 215
1. humility; 2. willingness; 3. love

page 219

page 221
1. The Christians; 2. They listened to the apostles' teaching, shared with each other, and worshipped together.; 3. They sold their possessions and used the money to help each other.; 4. They met together every day.; 5. They cooperated because they believed in God. God helped them love each other.

page 227
1. c; 2. b; 3. b; 4. a; 5. a; 6. b; 7. c.

page 231
1. D; 2. A; 3. C

page 233
trust, unselfish, love, kind, obey, joyful

page 237
Luke, Lydia, Joshua, fear

page 239
Jesus Christ is the same yesterday and today and forever.